*Complete Guide to
Accounting and Financial
Methods and Controls for
Service Businesses*

Complete Guide to
Accounting and Financial
Methods and Controls for
Service Businesses

Complete Guide to Accounting and Financial Methods and Controls for Service Businesses

by Richard Glickman

PRENTICE-HALL, INC.
Englewood Cliffs, N.J.

Prentice-Hall International, Inc., *London*
Prentice-Hall of Australia, Pty. Ltd., *Sydney*
Prentice-Hall of Canada, Ltd., *Toronto*
Prentice-Hall of India Private Ltd., *New Delhi*
Prentice-Hall of Japan, Inc., *Tokyo*
Prentice-Hall of Southeast Asia Pte. Ltd., *Singapore*
Whitehall Books, Ltd., *Wellington, New Zealand*

This publication is designed to provide accurate and
authoritative information in regard to the subject
matter covered. It is sold with the understanding that
the publisher is not engaged in rendering legal, accounting, or other professional service. If legal advice
or other expert assistance is required, the services of
a competent professional person should be sought.

*. . . From the Declaration of Principles jointly adapted
by a Committee of the American Bar Association and
a Committee of Publishers and Associations.*

Library of Congress Cataloging in Publication Data

Glickman, Richard
  Complete guide to accounting and financial methods
and controls for service businesses.

  Includes index.
  1. Financial statements. 2. Service industries
--Accounting. I. Title.
HF5681.B2G53   657'.83   78-32034
ISBN 0-13-159962-3

Printed in the United States of America

TO MY FAMILY

I want to dedicate this book to my family:

My wife, Barbara, who sustained and encouraged me while I spent long evening and weekend hours.

My children, Suzanne and Andrew, who had to be quiet while I wrote and who could not share my time.

My father, Max, who was my mentor and who inspired me to become a CPA.

My mother, Frances, who knew that some day I would write a book but who was not here when I began.

About the Author

Richard Glickman is a certified public accountant and a partner in the certified public accounting firm of Apt, Gluss, Glickman & Co. in New York City. He has nearly twenty years of public accounting experience and specializes in the accounting and financial requirements of small and large service businesses as well as trading and manufacturing enterprises. He has spoken before such organizations as the First Network of Affiliated Advertising Agencies and the National Association of Locksmith Suppliers, and has been published in professional journals. He received his B.A. from Pennsylvania State University, a B.S. in Engineering from the U.S. Naval Academy and a Master's degree from the Columbia University Graduate School of Business. He is a member of the American Institute of Certified Public Accountants (AICPA) and the New York State Society of Certified Public Accountants, and is president of the U.S. Naval Academy Association of New York.

A Word from the Author

This book addresses itself to the intelligent evaluation and presentation of financial statements of service businesses which operate without an inventory or where inventories are only incidental to their activities.

It explains how to prepare financial statements (financials) of service businesses accurately and why financials prepared along conventional lines may be misleading and possibly confusing.

To the best of my knowledge, no other book concerns itself only with financial and accounting methods and controls for service businesses.

Managers and accountants for service businesses need special tools and approaches to analyze their operations for profitable results as well as to present clearly to lending institutions, investors and others what is happening and what has happened.

Independent public accountants with clients in service businesses must know how to recognize their clients' problems, how to understand the problems, and know how to help solve them.

SPECIFIC BUSINESSES THE BOOK IS TAILORED TO

On the next page is a partial list of businesses whose requirements are covered in this work:

- Advertising agencies
- Broadcasting—radio and television
- Car washes
- Data processing services
- Funeral directors
- Hospitals
- Hotels and motels
- Laundries and dry cleaners
- Leasing
- Linen supply
- Nursing homes
- Personal services—other
- Real estate
- Sports and recreation
- Storage and warehousing
- Transportation
- Vending—coin operated

This book concerns itself with financial management of service businesses. It is a handbook of accounting methods and controls for such businesses. The thrust of this book is: "How Your Client Can Put More Into and Get More Out of His Financial Statements" to run the business more efficiently. Not only will this book explain what to do, it will explain what not to do and why not to do it.

EVEN PROFESSIONALS MISUNDERSTAND THE NEEDS OF SERVICE BUSINESSES

As an example, take this actual phone call to me from a partner in a regional public accounting firm. A client of mine had an investment in a service business audited by the caller. My client asked me to "look at" the financials. I found that the statement of changes in financial position was omitted. The financials included a *pro forma* balance sheet which created "working capital."

Clearly the financials were not in conformity with generally accepted accounting principles (GAAP).

Responding to my questioning, the partner of the large accounting firm explained that any reader of the financials who wanted to know could prepare his own statement of changes in financial position because the financials had comparative balance sheets.

It became clear from his statement that this book was written for public accountants and any other professionals who need to grasp the essential difference between service businesses and all other businesses.

SOLVING THE PROBLEM OF THE MISLEADING BALANCE SHEET

A successful, well-managed corporation which had been operating for about twenty years filed a registration statement a few years ago with the Securities and Exchange Commission. This corporation is primarily in a Service Business. It owns coin-operated vending machines which are placed in apartment houses. Tenants use these machines and pay for this service by depositing coins into the equipment.

When the original balance sheet was prepared and filed by this corporation, the S.E.C. asked if there was an "urgent need for funds." Furthermore, the S.E.C. said "working capital" appeared to be impaired. One of the questions raised by the S.E.C. was, "What creditors have demanded payments?" In this instance, the balance sheet was misleading to the S.E.C.

Why was the balance sheet misleading? Because the S.E.C. had applied the AICPA definition of "generally accepted accounting principles" to the balance sheet: Current liabilities exceeded current assets. Possibly, the S.E.C. thought that the Company sought to "go public" in order to avoid going bankrupt. How was this conclusion reached? The balance sheet was prepared in the conventional manner setting forth current assets and current liabilities for a business which properly has no such assets or liabilities. This book will illustrate in Chapter 1 how the Company could have avoided questioning and delay arising from the S.E.C. misunderstanding of Service Businesses and improper presentation of the financial statements.

WHY A SERVICE BUSINESS HAS NO CURRENT ASSETS OR LIABILITIES

Let us follow the reasoning as to why a service business has no current assets or current liabilities. To quote from Accounting Research and Terminology Bulletins, Final Edition, AICPA, 1961, pages 20-21:

> The ordinary operations of a business involve a circulation of capital within the current asset group. Cash is expended for materials, finished parts, operating supplies, labor and other factory services, and such expenditures are accumulated as inventory cost. Inventory costs, upon sale of the products to which such costs attach, are converted into trade receivables and ultimately into cash again. The average time intervening between the acquisition of materials or services entering this process and the final cash realization constitutes an operating cycle. A one-year time period is to be used as a basis for the segregation of current assets in cases where there are several operating cycles occurring within a year. However, where the period of the operating cycle is more than twelve months, as in, for instance, the tobacco, distillery, and lumber businesses, the longer period should be used. Where a particular business has no clearly defined operating cycle, the one-year rule should govern.

THE "INVENTORY" IS FIXED ASSETS

In service industries such as leasing or trucking, cash is primarily expended for "fixed assets," not for inventory. The ordinary operations of the business do not involve a circulation of capital within the current asset group. Fixed assets are leased with the expectation that the revenues so generated will have exceeded the cost of these assets and their related maintenance costs at the end of the useful lives of the fixed assets. Inventories may be acquired incidental to the maintenance of these fixed assets. These inventory costs in the leasing industries, unlike those of manufacturers, usually are not converted into receivables.

In service industries, receivables arise primarily from the leasing of fixed assets or from personal services rendered. When the customers pay cash immediately for services, as in the coin-operated segment of the vending industry, no receivables are generated. Fixed assets (vending machines) on location provide a service for which the consumer pays immediately in cash. This cash is not used immediately to acquire additional fixed assets.

Furthermore, there is no classic operating cycle in a service business. Certain periods during the year may have more business activity than in other periods. But this expansion and contraction of activity cannot be described as an "operating cycle" as we have just seen.

Therefore, the AICPA rule-of-thumb that a one-year time period is to be used as a basis of segregating current assets in cases where there are several operating cycles within a year does not relate to operations of service industies where there is neither an operating cycle nor an inventory (other than an incidental one).

This book is primarily for people who are financially oriented—accountants, controllers, treasurers, bankers, businessmen and others who want to be able to do more with the information available to them. This book explains how to construct and evaluate meaningful financials for service businesses. Chapter 6 shows how to control service businesses more effectively and maximize profits.

TOOLS FOR EVALUATION OF SERVICE BUSINESSES TO BE FOUND IN THIS BOOK

Financials are the tools of a businessman in a service business. He should be able to use these statements to create his business enterprise. When he has done this, he must be able to step away from his business and look objectively at it from time to time on a regular basis in order to make it grow and prosper. Too many businessmen cannot understand the financial statements which supposedly reflect the results of their efforts. Too many cannot interpret the economic posture that their businesses grow into. Even the professional whose task it is to evaluate service businesses is sometimes mislead by generally accepted accounting principles or by facts assembled in a conventional but misleading presentation.

There are additional measurement devices which the service businessman needs. These are performance evaluation analyses which, when developed and applied in conjunction with the financials, can produce results in decision making.

For example:

1. Net income per unit compared with budgeted income per unit.
2. Operational costs per unit compared with budgeted operational costs per unit.
3. Return on invested capital (ROI) as compared with projected ROI.
4. Gross receipts or sales per employee as compared with budgeted gross receipts or sales per employee.
5. Net income per employee compared with budgeted net income per employee.
6. Revenue-producing fixed assets per employee as compared with budgeted revenue-producing fixed assets per employee.
7. The concepts of planning, programming, budgeting, and controlling systems (PPBS).

The principles in this book could be applied to other service industries such as airlines, railroads, insurance companies, stockbrokers and others. However, these will not be discussed for two reasons. First, these businesses are regulated as to their accounting. Second, most accountants and auditors in small- and medium-sized public accounting firms are not called upon to prepare financials for these businesses.

Let us narrow our approach. This book will omit explanations and interpretations of financial statements of companies in those areas of business where inventory is a material income-producing factor. To illustrate, a wholesale distributor of food may believe that he is in a service business, but in actuality the inventory that he warehouses puts him into a non-service industry. His profit arises in buying and selling that food inventory. This trading activity is reflected in current assets where inventory becomes the major income-producing factor. Rising inventory prices and rising general price levels contribute to the profits of the business. If business conditions worsen and inventory values fall, the company may sustain losses. The service that the wholesaler here provides is that of a middleman. By our definition he is not in a service business, where service arises from personal services (attorneys, doctors, travel agents, dentists, architects, advertising agencies, and others), or services provided by the use of fixed assets (leased equipment, real estate, and so on) and no product is sold.

Many manufacturers sell the service concept to their customers, but because they sell a product they do not fall into our definition of a service business. One interesting question I had to ask myself was, "Is a bank a service business?" The answer is "no" because a bank sells cash which it must inventory for its customers.

Businessmen in service businesses do not describe their customers as "customers." They use such terms as "lessees" or "tenants." Professionals call their customers "patients" or "clients."

EXAMPLE OF A DISAPPEARING EQUITY PROBLEM AND WHERE TO FIND THE SOLUTION

A final example of a misleading evaluation before we get to the how-to specifics of this book is as follows:

The financials of a real estate corporation that owned and operated an apartment house were shown to me by a banker who complained that the corporation had substained losses such that the stockholder's equity or capital had disappeared. To use the banker's words, "The company was insolvent." I suggested to the banker that the bank send an appraiser to appraise the property, since the accumulated depreciation was much greater than the deficit. Furthermore, the real estate had actually appreciated in market value above its original cost. The diminution in stockholder's equity had occurred solely from rapid depreciation of the building. The balance sheet prepared in the conventional manner at cost did indeed indicate a problem. But the problem did not actually exist. Mere reading of the balance sheet was insufficient for the bank loan officer to arrive at an adequate value. Even the income statement did not reveal the true picture of the corporation's operations because it omitted an analysis of the profit available to amortize the corporate debt which consisted primarily of mortgages on the real estate. True analysis required that a funds statement or a statement of changes in financial position be evaluated, eliminating non-cash expenses and setting forth whether the earnings were adequate to repay the mortgage principal in accordance with its terms. Short-term bank loans may be valid if there is sufficient cash from operations to repay this debt. It is unusual for a real estate company to need short-term bank debt, but the need may arise from time to time depending upon the cash distribution policy and earnings. With proper analysis, if a banker then sees a working capital deficit or stockholders' capital deficiency, there would be no economic reason for him to turn down the loan.

Chapter 4 examines this problem in detail so that it may be avoided.

To sum up:

a) Financials of service businesses need separate treatment and analysis.

b) Financials of service businesses have one common characteristic—inventories are either non-existent or immaterial relative to the other assets of the enterprise.

RECAPITULATION

Now, to get to the essence of this book, it will explain:

1. How to prepare or recast Service Business financials.
2. How to interpret your client's Service Business financials.
3. What to do about real estate in non-real-estate businesses.
4. How to install controls to help your client maximize profits.
5. How the independent accountant can serve as the Treasurer of the Service client.
6. How to prepare and set up Service Business budgets for your client.
7. What special tax planning is needed by Service Businesses.
8. How to develop financial tools to build an organization.

Richard Glickman

Contents

19

1

How to Prepare Meaningful
Financial Statements for
the Service Business

SHORTCOMINGS OF CONVENTIONAL BALANCE SHEETS

Conventional balance sheets for service businesses tend to highlight the existence of a fact that really does not exist—working capital or, customarily, the apparent lack of it in a service business.

Service business financials should be tailored to the business. The essential points to bear in mind in balance sheet preparation are:

a. What assets generate the income?
b. How to reflect these assets most fairly and emphatically.

c. In what order should assets be set forth?

d. In personal service businesses, how should assets be segregated and presented?

e. Special information which should appear in footnotes.

f. Avoid classifying the accounts in the balance sheet.

Let us analyze the conventional balance sheet prepared by a company in the vending business which owns coin-operated washers and dryers on location in apartment houses, dormitories and other residential places where people bring their laundry to be washed. This company collects its revenues on a scheduled basis from a box installed in each washer and dryer.

The financials were filed a number of years ago in a registration statement with the Securities and Exchange Commission (SEC). Balance sheet accounts were classified into current and non-current. In its letter of comment to the company, the SEC asked a lot of questions relating to the lack of "working capital" because the current liabilities exceeded the current assets. Naturally, the registration was delayed and the securities were not sold as soon as the company had planned. The company attempted to defend its so-called lack of "working capital."

Illustration #1 shows the picture that was presented to the SEC.

In the four years ending on September 30, 19XX, the company's earnings were:

Current year	$ 245,000
Last year	$ 146,000
Three years prior	$ 87,000
Four years prior	$ 15,000

After going public the company's earnings were:

Year one	$ 300,000
Year two	$ 600,000
Year three	$ 700,000
Year four	$ 800,000
Year five	$1,100,000
Year six	$1,500,000

This is such a success story that it is difficult now to see why the SEC was so reluctant.

ILLUSTRATION #1

THE SERVICE BUSINESS, INC.

CONSOLIDATED BALANCE SHEET

ASSETS

	SEPTEMBER 30, 19XX
CURRENT ASSETS	
Cash	$ 192,025
Accounts receivable, less allowance for doubtful accounts $8,843	113,979
Inventories (Note 2)	212,166
Prepaid expenses	53,356
Sundry receivables	12,430
TOTAL CURRENT ASSETS	$ 583,956
REVENUE-PRODUCING EQUIPMENT—at cost (Note 3)	
Coin-operated laundry machines	$2,292,156
Less: Accumulated depreciation	1,233,139
TOTAL REVENUE-PRODUCING EQUIPMENT	$1,059,017
FIXED ASSETS—at cost (Note 3)	
Machinery, fixtures and equipment	$ 218,499
Autos and trucks	56,245
Leasehold improvements	49,546
	$ 324,290
Less: Accumulated depreciation and amortization	207,811
TOTAL FIXED ASSETS	$ 116,479
DEFERRED CHARGES (Note 1)	$ 273,539
INVESTMENTS (Note 4)	$ 31,486
DUE FROM OFFICERS-STOCKHOLDERS	$ 214,490
OTHER ASSETS	$ 123,499
TOTAL ASSETS	$2,402,466

See Notes to Financial Statements

ILLUSTRATION #1 (continued)

THE SERVICE BUSINESS, INC.

CONSOLIDATED BALANCE SHEET

LIABILITIES AND STOCKHOLDERS' EQUITY

	SEPTEMBER 30, 19XX
CURRENT LIABILITIES	
Notes payable—banks	$ 270,000
Accounts payable	177,215
Accrued liabilities:	
Commissions payable	119,485
Expenses and payroll	48,642
Taxes other than Federal tax on income	44,437
Estimated Federal income tax (Note 9)	178,633
Contribution to employee's profit sharing trust (Note (10)	30,000
Current portion of long-term debt	222,171
TOTAL CURRENT LIABILITIES	$1,090,583
LONG-TERM DEBT (Note 11)	
Notes payable, less amounts due within one year included in current liabilities	$ 230,308
CONTINGENT LIABILITIES (Note 12)	
STOCKHOLDERS' EQUITY (Note 1)	
Common Stock, $.10 par value	
Authorized 1,000,000 shares	
Issued 500,000 shares	50,000
Reserved for issuance on November 23, 19__	
27,000 shares	2,700
Capital in excess of par value	424,891
Retained earnings	603,984
TOTAL STOCKHOLDERS' EQUITY	$1,081,575
TOTAL LIABILITIES AND STOCKHOLDERS' EQUITY	$2,402,466

See Notes to Financial Statements

The mistake was that the company classified its assets and liabilities. No service business has current assets, current liabilities or working capital. Current assets and liabilities arise only when a company acquires assets to sell or manufactures assets to sell.

Service business revenue-producing assets do not consist of inventories to be sold. If service businesses do have inventories, these inventories are used in producing a service such as repairing revenue-producing assets. Such inventory amounts are not material, and are set forth in the balance sheet only incidentally.

The balance sheet in Illustration #1 reflected the following "working capital" deficiency:

Current assets	$ 583,956
Current liabilities	1,090,583
Working capital deficiency	$ (506,627)

What did this company do to overcome its supposed deficiency of $506,627 to make the SEC happy?

First, it agreed with its bankers to extend over a long-term period the obligations owing to the banks. This produced a *pro forma* reduction in "current liabilities" of $283,000.

Second, the officer-stockholders agreed to repay, upon registration, monies in the amount of $214,490 they had borrowed from the company.

Finally, the company was in a position to prepare a *pro forma* balance sheet reflecting the effect of the registration. Using updated numbers to March 31, of the next year, as required by the SEC, the *pro forma* was as follows:

Current assets	$ 1,067,008
Current liabilities	854,421
Working capital	$ 212,587

The reluctance of the SEC was overcome and the underwriters sold the securities of the company to the public. All problems could have been avoided if the balance sheet had been prepared as shown in Illustration #2 on pages 30 and 31.

ILLUSTRATION #2

THE SERVICE BUSINESS, INC.

CONSOLIDATED BALANCE SHEET

ASSETS

REVENUE-PRODUCING EQUIPMENT—at cost (Note 1)

Coin-operated laundry machines	$2,292,156
Less: Accumulated depreciation	1,233,139
REVENUE-PRODUCING EQUIPMENT—NET	$1,059,017
Cash	$ 192,025
Accounts receivable, less allowance for doubtful accounts $8,843	113,979
Inventories (Note 2)	212,166
Prepaid expenses	53,356
Due from officers-stockholders	214,490
	$ 786,016

FIXED ASSETS—at cost (Note 3)

Machinery, fixtures and equipment	$ 218,499
Autos and trucks	56,245
Leasehold improvements	49,546
	$ 324,290
Less: Accumulated depreciation and amortization	207,811
FIXED ASSETS—NET	$ 116,479
DEFERRED CHARGES (Note 1)	$ 273,539
INVESTMENTS (Note 4)	$ 31,486
OTHER ASSETS	$ 135,929
TOTAL ASSETS	$2,402,466

See Notes to Financial Statements

30

ILLUSTRATION #2 (continued)

THE SERVICE BUSINESS, INC.

CONSOLIDATED BALANCE SHEET

LIABILITIES AND STOCKHOLDERS' EQUITY

LIABILITIES

Notes payable—$222,171—due within one year (Note 11)	$ 452,479
Notes payable—banks	270,000
Accounts payable	177,215
Expenses and taxes accrued	242,564
Federal income tax payable (Note 9)	178,633
TOTAL LIABILITIES	**$1,320,891**

CONTINGENT LIABILITIES (Note 12)

STOCKHOLDERS' EQUITY (Note 1)

Common stock, $.10 par value	
Authorized 1,000,000 shares	
Issued 500,000 shares	$ 50,000
Reserved for issuance on November 23, 19X5	
27,000 shares	2,700
Capital in excess of par value	424,891
Retained earnings	603,984
TOTAL STOCKHOLDERS' EQUITY	**$1,081,575**
TOTAL LIABILITIES AND STOCKHOLDERS' EQUITY	**$2,402,466**

See Notes to Financial Statements

The "working capital" problem has been solved by not classifying the assets and liabilities.

Some lenders or security analysts faced with unclassified financials have gone shopping for "working capital" in the balance sheet even to the extent of recasting it into the classified form. If your client is subjected to this treatment, as an independent auditor you should explain that *cash* and not *"working capital"* is significant in a service business. Your attestation is to a fairly presented, *unclassified* balance sheet.

What the lender or security analyst needs to know is: Historically, has the company's cash position been adequate to meet its financial obligations? And, what will the company's cash position look like in the future? What will be the company's cash requirements and what will be the sources of its cash? Your client should forecast its cash needs and flows weekly, monthly, quarterly and annually. The statement of changes in financial position should be used as a tool. This statement will be discussed further and in greater detail in Chapter 3.

HOW A BANK WAS SATISFIED

Another smaller company in the same type of business had a problem borrowing from its bank. The management also failed to recognize its problem. However, this company decided to look harder for "current assets" and discovered a major asset previously unrecorded—uncollected cash.

At any given balance sheet date, sums of monies were still in the laundry's vending machines uncollected. The company proceeded to estimate this cash in machines based on average daily amounts collected per machine. The company then recorded the accrued amount as a current asset. The company also had to compute all related liabilities such as accrued commissions. When the smoke cleared, the "current assets" were substantially increased and to a much lesser extent the "current liabilities" were increased. The bank made the loan.

A proper analysis of the income statements of this company would have pointed up the error in the notion of deficit "working capital." Or, if the old "statement of sources and uses of funds," now the "statement of changes in financial position," had been prepared, both the bank and management would have seen the fallacy. Let us examine the income statements of this company. (See Illustration #3 on page 34.)

In the five-year period the company successfully managed to generate adequate cash except when it elected to grow at a greater rate in the fifth year. Then it had to resort to borrowing from a bank to finance its sizeable acquisitions of revenue-earning assets. This company was entitled to a line of credit from a bank to finance purchases of equipment. Its history of proper management is spread out in its record. It merely needed more money to expand than it was generating from its operations.

But the balance sheet continued to show a "deficit working capital" because the earnings were not being converted into "current assets." During the five-year period the company acquired revenue-earning equipment in the total amount of $746,000 while earning only a total of $413,000. Depreciation more than made up the necessary difference in the first four years.

Working capital here is meaningless. Obviously the company acquired many new locations in Year Five and needed to buy laundry machines for those locations. Fortunately, the company got its bank loan in Year Five and continued to prosper when the auditors pointed out to management that the balance sheet should be unclassified.

Of course, one might point out that this company could have resorted to financing other than bank financing. This course of action would have been more expensive. Why penalize a well-managed, healthy, young, prosperous, growing company because it is in a service business?

THE CASE OF THE CORRESPONDENCE SCHOOL

Not too many years ago I was retained to audit the financials of a small correspondence school.

The two owners were obviously primarily interested in making a lot of money and secondarily interested in education.

The financials of this service business were crudely pre-

ILLUSTRATION #3

	YEAR ONE	YEAR TWO	YEAR THREE	YEAR FOUR	YEAR FIVE	TOTAL
Sales	$650,000	$725,000	$825,000	$945,000	$1,130,000	$4,275,000
Operating expenses	$408,000	$457,000	$515,000	$584,000	$709,000	$2,673,000
Interest	42,000	38,000	35,000	31,000	26,000	172,000
Total	$450,000	$495,000	$550,000	$615,000	$735,000	$2,845,000
Income before depreciation	200,000	230,000	275,000	330,000	395,000	1,430,000
Depreciation	90,000	105,000	120,000	133,000	159,000	607,000
Income before income taxes	$110,000	$125,000	$155,000	$197,000	$236,000	$823,000
Income taxes	55,000	62,000	77,000	98,000	118,000	410,000
NET INCOME	$55,000	$63,000	$78,000	$99,000	$118,000	$413,000

The earnings of this company doubled in this five-year period. Nevertheless, in a service business we should analyze the rate of generation of cash.

	YEAR ONE	YEAR TWO	YEAR THREE	YEAR FOUR	YEAR FIVE	TOTAL
Net income	$55,000	$63,000	$78,000	$99,000	$118,000	$413,000
Depreciation	90,000	105,000	120,000	133,000	159,000	607,000
Total	$145,000	$168,000	$198,000	$232,000	$277,000	$1,020,000
Acquisition of revenue-earning assets	$100,000	$120,000	$135,000	$152,000	$239,000	$746,000
Amortization of debt	45,000	45,000	55,000	65,000	75,000	285,000
Total	$145,000	$165,000	$190,000	$217,000	$314,000	$1,031,000
CASH EXCESS OR DEFICIENCY	$ —	$3,000	$8,000	$15,000	$(37,000)	$(11,000)

pared. Polishing, reshaping and recasting was an important part of the auditors' task.

We studied their business. We studied the financials of their competitors. We were surprised and a little dismayed when we examined a very large successful school's balance sheet, which has been condensed in Illustration #4 on page 36.

Footnote No. 2 was a masterpiece of understatement, but it solved their "current asset" problem. Here is the first paragraph without a single word omitted:

> *Accounting Procedures:* For financial statement purposes revenue and expenses are recorded on the accrual basis of accounting although for income tax purposes portions of these items may be reported in a different period. The income taxes which will eventually be payable due to these timing differences, are charged against current income and included in accrued taxes-deferred at the time revenue and expenses are recorded for financial purposes. In accordance with current accounting practice the amounts due after one year have been included in current assets and current liabilities.

I underscored the last sentence because I understood it clearly—that the school included long-term receivables with their current assets. They apparently needed to do something to find working capital.

We wanted to know more about the first sentence of the footnote and what it meant. We called the company and spoke to the treasurer, a Mr. A.S. He was very happy to talk about his company, the largest in its field. He explained that, for financial statement purposes, the full sale amount is taken into revenue in the year of the sale; related expenses were accrued; and the company had a wonderful computer. The way Mr. A.S. explained things, all possible costs and expenses were matched against sales.

We could not accept his logic. How could the company record a sale if it takes three years to give a course? How could the company record a receivable in full from a student for a $595 course after receiving a down payment of only $25 and still give the student a two-year period to pay the balance?

We were assured that the wonderful computer took care of all the questions. The company knew, said Mr. A.S., how much

ILLUSTRATION #4

CONSOLIDATED BALANCE SHEET

JUNE 30, 19XX

ASSETS

CURRENT ASSETS

Cash and treasury bills	$ 2,510,000
Accounts receivable (Note 2)	18,370,000
Allowance for doubtful accounts	(3,154,000)
Lessons and materials in inventory	1,228,000
Prepaid expenses and other current assets	1,106,000
	$20,060,000

PROPERTY AND EQUIPMENT—at cost	$ 2,789,000
Less: Accumulated depreciation and amortization	950,000
	$ 1,839,000

OTHER ASSETS (Note 3)	$ 530,000
TOTAL ASSETS	$22,429,000

LIABILITIES

CURRENT LIABILITIES

Notes payable	$ 130,000
Accounts payable	1,922,000
Accrued salaries, commissions and tutorial costs	2,883,000
Accrued taxes—	
Current	925,000
Deferred (Note 2)	4,509,000
	$10,369,000

OTHER LIABILITIES (Notes 2, 4, and 7)	$ 1,004,000
	$11,373,000

SHAREHOLDERS' EQUITY (Note 8)

Common stock—$.02 par value	
Authorized—1,000,000	
Issued—500,000 shares	$ 10,000
Paid-in capital	9,000,000
Retained earnings	2,046,000
	$11,056,000

TOTAL LIABILITIES AND STOCKHOLDERS' EQUITY	$22,429,000

See Notes to Financial Statements

the course cost and immediately accrued the full amount. The company knew what its bad debts were going to be, based on its years of experience, and immediately accrued the full amount.

We felt a little bit better, but we did not have such a wonderful computer. We told our client that we were not going to let him take into income the full amount of his course which took about a year for a student to complete and pay for. Finally, we did not allow our client to classify the balance sheet.

A few years later, we were saddened to read in the financial obituary columns that friendly Mr. A.S. and his big publicly owned school had gone into bankruptcy. Subsequently we learned that the company had changed its accounting principles.

In retrospect, closer reading of Mr. A.S.'s statement of income would have pointed to the company's downfall by simply analyzing the following:

	Total Revenues (Million Dollars)	Provisions for Doubtful Accounts (Million Dollars)	Net Income (Million Dollars)
19X6	34.9	4.6	2.7
19X5	22.3	2.5	1.7
19X4	17.4	1.9	1.3
19X3	12.8	1.7	.9

In 19X7, the provision for doubtful accounts expense reached $6,000,000. When the 19X9 recession came along, the wonderful computer could not foresee that a lot of people would drop out of correspondence courses and that money would be tight in the money market. The provision for doubtful accounts expense could not be computed in advance so easily based on the company's experience. Net income turned into net loss.

It would have been more meaningful to take a different approach in preparing the financials. Income should have been recorded when the student paid for the course. Receivables should have been set forth only in the footnotes to the financials.

If the auditors had insisted on this principle of income realization, management would not have been in the posture of assuming it had a real asset of $15,000,000 of accounts receivable. Possibly the business would not have expanded so rapidly. The company would have been limited in its borrowings. Possibly it would still be alive today.

TIME AS AN INVENTORIABLE COST

Every principle must be evaluated for an exception to the rule. In accounting for service businesses there is one exception to be recognized in the preparation of balance sheets.

The exception is that where the service business sells time such as a personal service business, personal time is sold and inventoried. The business cycle begins when the service is performed. Time charges are accumulated as inventory. At a pre-arranged cut-off point such as completion of a service or at the end of a given time frame, the inventory is billed. The receivables thus generated are then converted back into cash. The cash pays for more time and the cycle begins again.

Personal service businesses selling time give rise to Principle No. 1—balance sheet accounts of time-selling service businesses should be classified. Receivables should be set up for billed costs as well as fees billed.

The fee or billing arrangement of a company in the time-selling service business must be analyzed carefully. The balance sheet should record each category of asset similar to non-service businesses except that inventory of work-in-process may consist of three sub-categories:

1. Inventory of time charges.
2. Inventory of out-of-pocket costs to be billed such as telephone or travel.
3. Inventory of costs to be billed specifically purchased in connection with the services rendered.

PERSONAL SERVICES

Personal services constitute a larger and larger segment of the service business population. My count to date of these businesses includes:

1. Accountants
2. Advertising agencies

3. Architects
4. Barbers
5. Beauticians
6. Brokers
    a. business
    b. custom house
    c. food
    d. insurance
    e. mortgage
    f. real estate
    g. securities
7 Computer record keeping
8. Dentists
9. Employment agencies
10. Engineers
11. Interior designers
12. Janitorial
13. Laboratories
14 Lawyers
15. Linen supply
16. Management consulting
17. Physicians
18. Public Relations
19. Repairs and maintenance
20. Schools
21. Studios
    a. art
    b. photographic
22. Telephone answering
23. Travel agencies

ATTORNEYS

Let us examine the balance sheet of a law firm prepared on an accrual basis.

This balance sheet demonstrates that personal service businesses do have "working capital." But this working capital does not arise from the selling or trading activity of a manufacturing, warehousing or retail enterprise. This personal service business sells time—people-time. In the balance sheet illustrated, client receivables is the largest single asset. Usually trade payables is the largest liability. If there is little or no long-term debt, the liabilities become minimal, such as accruals of taxes and expenses.

Many personal service businesses are conducted on a cash basis, especially if there is no indebtedness. Single practitioners, accountants, doctors, dentists, attorneys and others usually try to run their businesses in this fashion. Of course they fail to match revenues with expenses. As a result, they cannot evaluate their activities. Mistakenly they believe that they have to do this to minimize income taxes. Most personal service businesses are on a cash basis for income tax purposes. For management purposes, the business should be adjusted to an accrual basis. The smaller the business, the simpler the adjustment.

As shown in Illustration #5, the inventory of work-in-progress consists of fees receivable at either standard or adjusted rates. Expenses incurred on behalf of and billed to the client should be charged to a Disbursements receivable account.

INSURANCE BROKERS

Some personal service businesses may have to make payments on behalf of their customers or may elect to do so. Insurance brokers, for example, may advance premiums to an insurance company because their customers have not remitted either the premium amount or the fee. The typical insurance broker takes his fees into income when the premiums are due and payable. It is at that moment that he earns his commission from the company. If he hasn't collected from his customer, he can pay the premium out of his own funds on behalf of the customer.

Insurance brokers function in a dual capacity. They act as agents for insureds in the placing of insurance and for the companies in the collection of premiums. Because they are in a fiduciary position they must segregate in special cash accounts the premiums they have collected and are holding for the companies.

There is another concept prevalent in the insurance broker-

ILLUSTRATION #5

WELLINGTON AND LEVY, ESQS.

BALANCE SHEET

JUNE 30, 19XX

ASSETS

CURRENT ASSETS

Cash	$ 89,000
Marketable securities—temporary investments	41,000
Accounts receivable—clients	438,000
Inventory of work in progress—unbilled	86,000
Disbursements receivable	21,000
Disbursements	4,000
TOTAL CURRENT ASSETS	$679,000

FIXED ASSETS

Office equipment (less accumulated depreciation $9,000)	$ 38,000
Furniture and furnishings (less accumulated depreciation $47,000)	199,000
Automobile (less accumulated depreciation $7,000)	23,000
TOTAL	$260,000
Deposits	4,000
Deferred charges	17,000
TOTAL ASSETS	$960,000

LIABILITIES AND PARTNERSHIP CAPITAL

LIABILITIES

CURRENT LIABILITIES

Notes payable—bank	$ 65,000
Current portion—long-term debt	21,000
Accounts payable	79,000
Taxes and expenses accrued	16,000
Partners' drawing	140,000
TOTAL CURRENT LIABILITIES	$321,000
Non-current portion—long-term debt	118,000
TOTAL LIABILITIES	$439,000
PARTNERSHIP CAPITAL	521,000
TOTAL LIABILITIES AND PARTNERSHIP CAPITAL	$960,000

41

age business. Income is reflected on the cash rather than accrual basis. Income is recorded when premiums are collected and expenses are not accrued. This concept has the practical effect of deferring income taxes. However, there is inadequate matching of revenues and expenses. If income taxes are a significant problem the books could be kept on a cash basis and the financial statements prepared on an accrual basis. This procedure necessitates additional record keeping.

If you are auditing an insurance broker, recommend that his financials be prepared on an accrual basis. Only then can income measurement be accomplished properly.

Balance sheets of insurance brokers are usually classified and contain three special debit accounts peculiar to the business.

Cash—Premiums Held for Insurance Companies
Due for Premiums Advanced for Customers
Accounts Receivable—Premiums Billed to Customers

Also, there should be recorded as a contra to the above Cash account, the following special credit account:

Due to Insurance Companies for Premiums Collected

The insurance broker is selling a service, but his fees are related to the size and nature of the insurance he places. Although he only has time to sell and may work on placing a piece of insurance over an extended time frame, he cannot accumulate his time like an attorney, dentist, doctor, accountant or other professional. His time is not inventoriable.

MORTGAGE BROKERS AND MORTGAGE BANKERS

In the mortgage brokeraging business, the typical brokerage company will arrange what is known as a "warehousing" line of credit from a bank. The mortgage broker can hold the mortgage himself for a short period of time using these warehouse funds from the bank until he has favorably placed the mortgage with a financial institution. Some mortgage brokers are also in the business of servicing mortgages for financial institutions. They perform the task of collection and follow-up. Usually once a month they remit the total they have collected with a statement of account balances for each of the mortgages they are servicing.

SERVICE BUSINESS INVENTORIES

Inventories do appear on balance sheets of personal service businesses. Usually these inventories are only incidental to the business. Office supplies make up many inventories. Dental supplies, barbers' supplies, janitorial supplies, medical supplies—all are typically incidental to the personal services involved.

Inventories are more important but still not a major item in the following fields:

1. Funeral directors
2. Hospitals and nursing homes
3. Hotels and motels
4. Leasing
5. Television and radio broadcasting

Funeral directors' inventories fall into three categories: supplies used for embalming and preparations for the burial; office supplies; and caskets, which are sold as part of the total cost of the funeral.

Hospitals and nursing homes maintain inventories of food, janitorial supplies, office supplies, medical and housekeeping supplies including linen. None of these items are sold except that patients are charged for medical supplies of certain types.

Hotels and motels maintain janitorial supplies, office supplies, and housekeeping supplies including linen. The restaurant part of a hotel's operations is not a service business.

Leasing companies usually keep inventories of spare parts of whatever it is they are leasing plus office supplies. Truck leasing companies keep spare parts for truck repairs. Equipment leasing companies keep inventories of parts needed for repairs and maintenance. Many leasing companies have no inventories of spare parts. These companies are really in the financing business only. Whatever they own and lease must be repaired and maintained either by another company or by the customer himself. Many banks run separate leasing companies in order to provide this type of financing for their customers and depositors.

Television and radio broadcasting stations inventory office supplies and spare parts for equipment as well as studio props and a library of tapes or records.

MISLEADING CREDIT ANALYSIS

Many businesses belong to trade groups that encourage standardization and uniformity of accounting. One of the problems facing service businesses today is that reputable organizations are gathering financial data that are misleading to credit analysts. There are companies in the credit business as well as industry groups accumulating financial data in selected industries.

If a bank loan officer is approached by a potential customer in a service business, that loan officer may and usually does refer to industry-wide financial information gathered by various disseminating organizations. As soon as he looks at the balance sheet data he has in his library, the banker sees that the companies in that particular service business generally have "working capital" deficits. This is only true because they really have no working capital at all. The data-gathering organization has made no distinction in tabulating its information between a retailer, wholesaler, manufacturer, or service business. All of the financial statements in all phases of business are reduced to a simple form. This form which demands that assets be classified into current and non-current is run through a computer. The figures are programmed into working capital and deficit working capital.

The banker may very well be reluctant to make the loan that the service business seeks, and to which it is really entitled, when he sees that his customer's competitors all have "working capital" deficits. The independent public accounting firm should consult with the client seeking a bank loan to explain why there is no deficit "working capital."

One of the big New York banks advertised recently, "If your loan officer won't make the loan, try another loan officer." The solution is to stop conforming service business financials to the financials of manufacturers, wholesalers and retailers.

WHY REAL ESTATE FOOLS MOST BUSINESSMEN

I live in a co-operative apartment house. Each year the auditors audit the financials and prepare a splendid report without classifying current assets and current liabilities.

The only business the co-op has is managing the building. Despite the auditors' statement, the part-time voluntary treasurer, who is also a tenant in the co-op, prepares his own analysis of what happened during the past year. He recasts the financials and proudly points to the growing "working capital."

As I see it, this money is being properly set aside so that the co-op will have cash available for emergencies or for major capital improvements. When the day arrives to pay for some large new piece of equipment, I am sure that the treasurer will deplore the decline in his "working capital." I am also sure that the treasurer has a business of his own that demands working capital such as a manufacturer where working capital is monitored and husbanded.

The treasurer is like a fish out of water. Obviously service businesses are foreign to him. Yet he insists on looking for "working capital" in a real estate business. He takes such pains to explain why the "working capital" increased, but instead he should only be looking at the cash flow.

Many successful businessmen wake up one fine day to find that they have added another business to the one they originally started. This happens to the retailer who buys the real estate where he has been the tenant or the wholesaler who buys the warehouse. Suddenly this businessman is in a service business. If he starts looking for "working capital" in his new business he is only going to fool himself.

Chapter 4 takes some of the mystery out of real estate financials. If you have clients that are not in service businesses, for example retailing, wholesaling or manufacturing, and your client is seeking to purchase its own real estate or has purchased its own real estate, you should examine Chapter 4.

How do real estate financials look if one seeks "working capital" in the financials? Let us examine Illustration #6, which shows a typical apartment house residential balance sheet prepared in accordance with generally accepted accounting principles.

Current liabilities in the amount of $227,000 exceed current assets by $37,000. On the brink of insolvency? Hardly! The debt-to-equity ratio is approximately five to one. Unusual? Just the opposite. This is typical real estate leverage.

The balance sheet alone cannot tell the tale. Most important is the question, "Does the depreciation and net income exceed the required mortgage amortization payments?" Another important question related to the first, "What is the occupancy rate?" When a low percentage of the apartments are vacant, the rent roll provides the funds to operate the building and amortize the mortgage debt.

Well-managed buildings such as the aforementioned co-op usually generate excess cash to stockpile in the event of an emergency.

The statement of changes in financial position and income statement together indicate the value of a real estate investment.

The relationship of the debt structure to the cash flow is most significant. The length of the mortgage and the interest and amortization rates are very important. If a mortgage falls due and cannot be extended or renewed, then the owner of the real estate must either obtain other debt financing, place his own funds into the real estate to replace the debt or lose his property in a foreclosure of the mortgage.

WAREHOUSING AND STORAGE FINANCIALS

Recently I reviewed the financials of a successful warehousing and storage company. Profits and cash generation were excellent. If the balance sheet were classified as to current and non-current it would have reflected a deficit working capital in the amount of $68,000, arrived at as follows:

Current assets	$1,581,000
Current liabilities	1,649,000
Deficit working capital	$ (68,000)

ILLUSTRATION #6

ONE PARK STREET CORP.

BALANCE SHEET—DECEMBER 31, 19XX

ASSETS

CURRENT ASSETS

Cash	$	49,000
Tenants' accounts receivables		19,000
Inventories of fuel and supplies		13,000
Temporary investments		86,000
Prepaid insurance and other expenses		23,000
TOTAL CURRENT ASSETS	$	190,000

Real Estate—Note 1

Land	$	75,000
Building (Less accumulated depreciation $180,000)		711,000
Furniture, furnishing and equipment (less accumulated depreciation $18,000)		38,000
TOTAL REAL ESTATE	$	824,000
Deferred charges—Note 2	$	22,000
Organization expenses unamortized	$	3,000
TOTAL ASSETS		$1,039,000

LIABILITIES AND STOCKHOLDERS' EQUITY

LIABILITIES

CURRENT LIABILITIES

Mortgage payable—current portion—Note 3	$	61,000
Accounts payable		34,000
Tenants' security deposits payable		42,000
Taxes and expenses accrued		38,000
Income taxes payable—current		52,000
TOTAL CURRENT LIABILITIES	$	227,000
Mortgage payable—non-current portion—Note 3		641,000
TOTAL LIABILITIES	$	868,000

STOCKHOLDERS' EQUITY

Capital stock—authorized, issued and outstanding 5,000 shares—$10 par value	$	50,000
Retained earnings		121,000
TOTAL STOCKHOLDERS' EQUITY	$	171,000
TOTAL LIABILITIES AND STOCKHOLDERS' EQUITY		$1,039,000

See Notes to Financial Statements

Meaningless? Let us examine Illustration #7 to see how the financials were set forth.

Here is a service business with total assets of almost $9.5 million. The inventory is only $12,000. The current asset concept is meaningless.

What is meaningful? The two largest asset categories—real estate and trucks—are the essence of this business, comprising nearly eighty percent of the total assets.

Look at the real estate values on the books:

Land	$ 470,000
Building (net)	5,511,000
	$5,981,000

Total mortgages payable amount to $6,161,000. This exceeds the book value of the real estate by $180,000. Obviously the real estate values have increased above the book values and the company has refinanced its mortgages. The financial institutions holding the mortgages could see that the income statement and statement of changes in financial position warranted a refinancing.

Net Income	$ 391,000
Add back: depreciation	627,000
	$1,018,000
Long-term debt to be amortized within one year	481,000
Funds available for annual operation	$ 537,000

The financial institutions also did their own appraisal of the real estate. Apparently the value they placed on the real estate was higher than its book value. The company, recognizing this differential, sought and obtained a higher mortgage. The additional cash thus obtained was reinvested into the business.

ILLUSTRATION #7

GENERAL STORAGE AND WAREHOUSE CORP.

BALANCE SHEET—DECEMBER 31, 19XX

ASSETS

CURRENT ASSETS
Cash	$ 587,000
Accounts Receivable (less allowance for doubtful accounts $29,000)—Note 1	878,000
Inventory	12,000
Prepaid expenses	90,000
Loans receivable employees	10,000
Sundry	4,000
TOTAL CURRENT ASSETS	$1,581,000

FIXED ASSETS—Note 2
Trucks (less allowance for depreciation $493,000)	1,379,000
Equipment (less allowance for depreciation $49,000)	226,000

Real Estate
Land	470,000
Building (less allowance for depreciation of $1,808,000)	5,511,000
TOTAL FIXED ASSETS	$7,586,000

Deferred charges	$ 235,000
Deposits	23,000
TOTAL ASSETS	$9,425,000

LIABILITIES AND STOCKHOLDERS' EQUITY

LIABILITIES
CURRENT LIABILITIES
Current portion—long-term debt—Note 3	$ 481,000
Accounts payable	332,000
Income taxes payable	240,000
Taxes and expenses accrued	596,000
TOTAL CURRENT LIABILITIES	$1,649,000

Mortgage payable—non-current portion—Note e	5,680,000
TOTAL LIABILITIES	$7,329,000

STOCKHOLDERS' EQUITY
Capital stock 1,000,000 shares issued and outstanding $1.00 par value	$ 200,000
Retained earnings	1,896,000
TOTAL STOCKHOLDERS' EQUITY	$2,096,000
LIABILITIES AND STOCKHOLDERS' EQUITY	$9,425,000

See Notes to Financial Statements

The independent accountant or his client should be able to prepare a forecast indicating the following:

Current Assets—December 31	$1,581,000
Additional cash to be generated from next year's operations	537,000
TOTAL	$2,118,000
Current Liabilities—December 31	1,649,000
Working Capital one year later	$ 469,000

The deficit of $68,000 has reversed itself to the extent of $469,000 on a *pro forma* basis one year later. It should be obvious to the public accountant and his client that the whole idea of working capital presentation is meaningless.

What is meaningful is the present rate of cash generation. All liabilities excluding mortgages as of December 31 amounted to $1,168,000. Assuming the present rate of cash generation will continue, a *pro forma* statement of changes in financial position indicates that this debt will be satisfied entirely in a little more than two years. No liabilities will remain other than the mortgage. At that time the corporation will be able to prepay this if it so desires.

As the independent public accountant for a warehousing and storage client, you should not classify the balance sheet. You should insist that your client's interim and annual financials, whether prepared by management or by you, include a statement of changes in financial position. Chapter 3 presents various approaches to be used in designing formats for a meaningful analysis of this statement.

HYBRID BUSINESSES

Some businessmen are in two businesses simultaneously such as locksmiths who retail locks as well as provide a service of repair and/or installation. Since inventories are significant, these hybrid businesses should classify their balance sheets. Income statements should be broken down by function.

PRACTICAL PLANNING CONSIDERATIONS
FOR FINANCIAL STATEMENT PREPARATION

1. Balance sheets for service businesses should not classify current assets and current liabilities because there are none in service businesses.
2. Inventories usually are not significant in service businesses because they are not sold in the normal course of business.
3. The concept of "working capital" or "deficit working capital" is meaningless in all service businesses except personal service businesses.
4. Personal service balance sheets should be classified because the inventory that they pay for is time—people-time. Time is accumulated as unbilled receivables or inventory of work-in-progress.
5. Real estate ownership fools most businessmen who are not in the real estate business if they try to find "working capital."
6. The statement of changes in financial position and income statement are more significant than the balance sheet for purposes of financial analysis in service businesses.

2

Balance Sheet Analysis: Putting the Balance Sheet to Work as a Profit Tool

HOW TO PREPARE BALANCE SHEET TREND ANALYSIS

At the end of each month, your client or your company closes its books and a set of financials is prepared. The profit or loss for the period is determined. The changes in financial position are determined and the balance sheet sets forth the new posture of the company at that date.

Query: To what other balance sheet should that balance sheet be compared? Conventional balance sheets use the **year-ago-same-date** approach. Interim financials should also be related to the balance sheet as of day one of the current fiscal year. Interim financials reflect interim earnings and interim changes

53

in financial position. Therefore, meaningful interim financials should contain three separate but related balance sheets as follows:

a. Month end—current year
b. Month end—year-ago-same-date
c. Beginning date—current fiscal year

This approach to balance sheet presentation is equally relevant to companies not on calendar quarters that use four thirteen-week quarters broken down into a sequence of weeks—groups of four weeks, four weeks and five weeks.

Balance sheet analysis should be tailored to each company's needs. Some managements like to compare the month-end balance sheet with the prior month. Some like to compare the end of the quarterly period with the end of the prior quarterly period as well as with the beginning of the fiscal year. A rapidly growing or changing company will not learn as much by comparing the current month-end with the month-end year-ago-same-date because of the very considerable change in the posture of the business.

Preparation of the interim or annual balance sheets should be the first step in putting the balance sheet to work. The second step should be the preparation of balance sheet trends for management analysis. Relationships of items within the balance sheet can be viewed in two ways: the account can be compared to itself over a time frame and it can be compared to the other items individually or in total. Before comparisons are prepared, it is important that the time frame be determined. Usually an annual and a quarterly time series is important. Some companies believe that a monthly series over a two-, three-, four- or five-year time span is meaningful. Finally, it is necessary to decide which information is to be monitored and why.

Trend analysis is more than simply reviewing a series of balance sheets. Significant items should appear separately in each balance sheet. Accounts of little importance or accounts not numerically material should be grouped and presented in total. Where meaningful, a sub-group may be analyzed in trend separately from the balance sheet trend. Usually this is done in a separate report or document. Illustration #1 on pages 56 to 59 shows a series of annual balance sheets of one corporation, both in dollars and expressed in a percent of total. A four-year time frame is presented because in the next succeeding year the company acquired the other 50% of its domestic subsidiary and consolidated the balance sheet.

The auditor or client has set forth the salient fact of this business. Immaterial assets are grouped into the "Other Asset" category. Schedules should be prepared to support in detail the accounts summarized. For example, in Illustration #1 there should be at least four supporting schedules:

1. Prepaid expenses and taxes
2. Due from officers and stockholders
3. Investments
4. Other assets

Security analysts will not look for and the SEC has no way to see that there is a deficit of "working capital." Comparative balance sheets will highlight the growth and implementation of "Revenue-Producing Equipment."

This balance sheet is unclassified. All significant assets should be described in the footnotes as well as related accounting principles. Market value of investments also should be reflected. Where the assets are leveraged and encumbered, the related liabilities should be described in detail. Since cash may be in the laundry machines rather than in the bank, a proper explanation of this asset is in order. Cash set forth in the balance sheet is not readily available since it must be collected from the machines. I consider this as special additional information needed to analyze this balance sheet.

Now let us look at the Liabilities and Stockholders' Equity section of the balance sheet as it should be presented.

The four-year trend shows an overview of corporate activity. Obviously, earnings are being retained and reinvested into an ever-increasing expansion of Revenue-Producing Assets. Corporate debt has not been a significant factor in this expansion, as evidenced by the fact that total liabilities have increased in the amount of $571,000 whereas total assets have increased

ILLUSTRATION #1

THE COIN-OPERATOR CORP.

BALANCE SHEET—SEPTEMBER 30, 19XX

ASSETS

ASSETS	19X5	19X4	19X3	19X2
Cash	$ 611,363	$ 602,631	$ 389,959	$ 557,239
Percentage	11.9%	14.7%	11.1%	17.1%
Accounts receivable—net allowance for doubtful accounts	116,819	166,584	106,295	79,153
Percentage	2.3%	4.1%	3.0%	2.4%
Inventories	432,439	369,397	396,682	277,347
Percentage	8.4%	9.0%	11.4%	8.5%
Prepaid expenses and taxes	37,409	49,262	27,564	31,217
Percentage	0.8%	1.2%	0.8%	1.0%
Sundry receivables	13,313	37,709	28,050	13,424
Percentage	0.3%	0.9%	0.8%	0.4%
Revenue-producing equipment—at cost less accumulated depreciation	2,607,000	1,894,214	1,643,318	1,422,944
Percentage	50.7%	46.3%	47.0%	43.7%
Fixed assets—machinery, fixtures, transportation equipment, leasehold improvements—at cost, less accumulated depreciation	257,613	121,155	114,814	116,527
Percentage	5.0%	3.0%	3.3%	3.6%

ILLUSTRATION #1 (continued)

THE COIN-OPERATOR CORP.

BALANCE SHEET—SEPTEMBER 30, 19XX

ASSETS

OTHER ASSETS	19X5	19X4	19X3	19X2
Investment in and advances to domestic subsidiary unconsolidated	$ 437,698	$ 455,878	$ 437,759	$ 323,767
Percentage	8.5%	11.2%	12.5%	10.0%
Advances to foreign affiliates	25,432	22,040	22,821	96,886
Percentage	0.4%	0.5%	0.7%	3.0%
Cost in excess of net assets of wholly owned subsidiaries at acquisition	438,377	274,730	274,730	274,730
Percentage	8.5%	6.7%	7.9%	8.5%
Deferred charges	139,723	82,026	36,456	31,876
Percentage	2.7%	2.0%	1.0%	1.0%
Miscellaneous	27,931	14,578	18,795	27,505
Percentage	0.5%	0.4%	0.5%	0.8%
TOTAL OTHER ASSETS	$1,069,161	$ 849,252	$ 790,561	$ 754,764
Percentage	20.6%	20.8%	22.6%	23.3%
TOTAL ASSETS	$5,145,117	$4,090,204	$3,497,243	$3,252,615
	100.0%	100.0%	100.0%	100.0%

See Accompanying Notes

ILLUSTRATION #1 (continued)

THE COIN-OPERATOR CORP.

BALANCE SHEET—SEPTEMBER 30, 19XX

LIABILITIES AND STOCKHOLDERS' EQUITY	19X5	19X4	19X3	19X2
Notes payable	$ 896,519	$ 643,556	$ 600,256	$ 816,853
Percentage	17.4%	15.7%	17.2%	25.1%
Accounts payable	219,918	178,976	251,911	111,053
Percentage	4.3%	4.4%	7.2%	3.4%
Federal income tax accrued	392,311	455,940	203,415	211,589
Percentage	7.6%	11.1%	5.8%	6.5%
Other taxes and expenses accrued	545,085	392,678	363,633	368,409
Percentage	10.6%	9.6%	10.4%	11.3%
Deferred income taxes	25,281	—	—	—
Percentage	0.5%	—	—	—
TOTAL LIABILITIES	$2,079,114	$1,671,150	$1,419,215	$1,507,904
Percentage	40.4%	40.8%	40.6%	46.3%

Contingent Liabilities

ILLUSTRATION #1 (continued)

THE COIN-OPERATOR CORP.

BALANCE SHEET—SEPTEMBER 30, 19XX

STOCKHOLDERS' EQUITY	19X5	19X4	19X3	19X2
Capital stock	$ 86,050	$ 85,250	$ 85,250	$ 85,250
Percentage	1.7%	2.1%	2.4%	2.6%
Capital contributed in excess of par value	746,041	678,841	678,841	678,841
Percentage	14.5%	16.6%	19.4%	20.9%
Retained earnings	2,406,190	1,827,241	1,313,937	980,620
Percentage	46.8%	44.7%	37.6%	30.2%
	$3,238,281	$2,591,332	$2,078,028	$1,744,711
	63.0%	63.4%	59.4%	53.7%
Less: Treasury stock	172,278	172,278	—	—
Percentage	3.4%	4.2%	—	—
TOTAL STOCKHOLDERS' EQUITY	$3,066,003	$2,419,054	$2,078,028	$1,744,711
Percentage	59.6%	59.2%	59.4%	53.7%
TOTAL LIABILITIES AND STOCKHOLDERS' EQUITY	$5,145,117	$4,090,204	$3,497,243	$3,252,615
Percentage	100.0%	100.0%	100.0%	100.0%

59

$1,892,000. Revenue-Producing Assets increased in the amount of $1,184,056 and as a percentage of total assets from 44% to 51%.

Overall long-range corporate analysis can be made with this type of trend information. For example, why has management not seen fit to acquire Revenue-Producing Assets by debt financing? As another example, is too much cash invested in inventory, which in service businesses really does not produce revenues?

Trend analysis over short periods of time using monthly balance sheets is informative in day-to-day type decision making versus the long-range type presented in Illustration #1. Usually the most meaningful time frame for this type of analysis consists of twenty-four monthly balance sheets set forth both in dollars and as a percent of total assets and liabilities and stockholders' equity.

Preparation of this kind of trend analysis should be on a different level than the annual trend. Monthly balance sheets should be more detailed, with less grouping of accounts than annual balance sheets. Management should decide which asset and liability monthly measurements are most meaningful.

Let us look at the cash account in Illustration #2 using two twelve-month time frames in dollars (thousands omitted) and cash as a percentage of total assets. Amounts are stated at the month-end.

ILLUSTRATION #2
YEAR ONE
(in thousands of dollars)

OCT.	NOV.	DEC.	JAN.	FEB.	MAR.	APR.	MAY	JUN.	JUL.	AUG.	SEP.
$ 717	810	721	802	891	733	925	994	868	892	946	982
9.1%	9.3	8.7	9.1	9.4	8.4	9.3	9.8	9.1	9.3	9.9	10.6%

YEAR TWO

OCT.	NOV.	DEC.	JAN.	FEB.	MAR.	APR.	MAY	JUN.	JUL.	AUG.	SEP.
$ 998	1,075	987	1,034	1,116	940	1,157	1,210	1,083	1,237	1,292	1,320
10.1%	10.3	9.7	10.1	10.8	9.6	10.9	11.2	10.4	11.6	11.8	12.2%

An analysis of the above trend should be profitable for management. The company should prepare this information and do its own analysis. Some questions to be asked of management here are:

1. Why was cash allowed to accumulate, nearly doubling in a two-year period?
2. Why is an increasing percent of the company's assets invested in cash rather than in revenue-producing assets?
3. Can borrowings be prepaid to reduce interest cost?
4. Should cash be paid out to stockholders in the form of increased dividends?
5. How much surplus cash has been invested in securities such as certificates of deposit, treasury bills or bankers acceptances which produce income?

HOW TO SAVE EVALUATION TIME

There is another way to present the two twelve-month time frames which will save management evaluation time. The idea is to use the management-by-exception approach as follows in Illustration #3.

ILLUSTRATION #3
(in thousands of dollars)

	OCT.	NOV.	DEC.	QUARTER CHANGE	JAN.	FEB.	MAR.	QUARTER CHANGE	CUM. CHANGE
$	717	810	721	+4$	802	891	733	−69	+16$
%	9.1	9.3	8.7	−.4%	9.1	9.4	8.4	− .7	− .7%

	APR.	MAY	JUN.	QUARTER CHANGE	CUM. CHANGE	JUL.	AUG.	SEP.	QUARTER CHANGE	CUM. CHANGE
$	925	994	868	−57	+151	892	946	982	+90	+265
%	9.3	9.8	9.1	− .2	0	9.3	9.9	10.6	1.3	1.5

Management should watch these changes only. Here the first and second quarter change columns do not show any significant amounts. The cumulative change column at the end of the third fiscal quarter shows a dollar increase of $151,000, representing an approximate increase of twenty-one percent in dollars. Management analysis should begin with this signal on June 30. Some companies set parameters to watch for month-to-month changes. Illustration #4 uses this management-by-exception concept.

ILLUSTRATION #4
YEAR ONE
(in thousands of dollars)

OCT.	NOV.	CHANGE	DEC.	CHANGE	CUM. CHANGE	JAN.	CHANGE	CUM. CHANGE
$717	810	+93	721	−89	+4	802	+81	+85

FEB.	CHANGE	CUM. CHANGE	MAR.	CHANGE	CUM. CHANGE	APR.	CHANGE	CUM. CHANGE
$891	+91	+174	733	−158	+16	925	+192	+208

MAY	CHANGE	CUM. CHANGE	JUN.	CHANGE	CUM. CHANGE	JUL.	CHANGE	CUM. CHANGE
$994	+69	+277	868	−126	+151	892	+24	+175

AUG.	CHANGE	CUM. CHANGE	SEP.	CHANGE	CUM. CHANGE
$946	+54	+229	982	+36	$+265

In this illustration there is a major shift from March to April which is signaled earlier than in Illustration #3 which produced a major signal at the end of the April-to-June quarter. Some companies will prepare, in addition to Illustration #4, a series in which both the change and cumulative change are expressed in percent. For example, instead of $+93 in the Oct.-Nov. change column, the change would have been set forth at +12.9%

In service businesses, evaluating cash movements is as important as evaluating inventories in other types of businesses such as manufacturing, wholesaling and retailing. As cash accumulates in a service business it can be used to acquire more revenue-producing assets when it reaches certain levels of excess. Short-term or long-term loans can be prepaid with excess cash.

Therefore, it is usually more productive when management prepares a series using dollar amounts rather than percentages, although some companies may prefer a combination-type approach.

TIME SERIES PARAMETERS

Certain service businesses afford little opportunity to put the balance sheet to work on a month-to-month basis because change occurs infrequently in the balance sheet. For example, some businesses such as real estate investment and television and radio station operations afford little or no short-run change in the assets that generate revenues. An operator of an apartment house or a taxpayer usually makes a single investment which does not recur. Even expenditures for major renovation are spaced over long time frames. Balance sheet trends in these businesses should be charted and analyzed quarterly and annually.

In a business such as leasing, where revenue-earning assets are changing continuously, month-to-month trend analysis is important. Here monthly acquisitions are made and leases are written. This type of change must be monitored closely.

A fascinating trend line to watch and learn from is the change in liabilities. Once a radio station goes into profitable operation there should be a continuous decline in long-term liabilities. Projected out, good management can see a cash buildup. This could be used for increased salaries, dividends to stockholders, improvement or replacement of facilities or possibly another station acquisition.

In real estate investment a projected long-term reduction of mortgage liabilities could lead to a refinancing. A tax-free cash windfall may be in order. This concept is explained more fully in Chapter 4.

The truck leasing business must take a different approach in analyzing balance sheet trends. The key to liability trend analysis is the means whereby trucks are financed by the leasing company. Indebtedness arising solely from the purchase of trucks and placing them out on lease should grow in a trend line relative to the asset trend line growth. Retention of earnings reduces financing requirements.

PERSONAL SERVICE BALANCE SHEET TREND ANALYSIS

Professional organizations or even individual practitioners such as attorneys, architects, accountants, doctors, dentists and others have much to learn from trend analysis. A trend may show that in specific months there is usually a recurring cash shortage. Later in the year there may be excess cash. Prudent management will plan to borrow during the period with inadequate or insufficient cash. When the cycle shows excess fund generation, the loan is repaid.

Heavy capital asset purchases should be financed preferably with a long-term debt arrangement. Such debt must be

ILLUSTRATION #5
CASH RECEIPTS
(IN THOUSANDS)

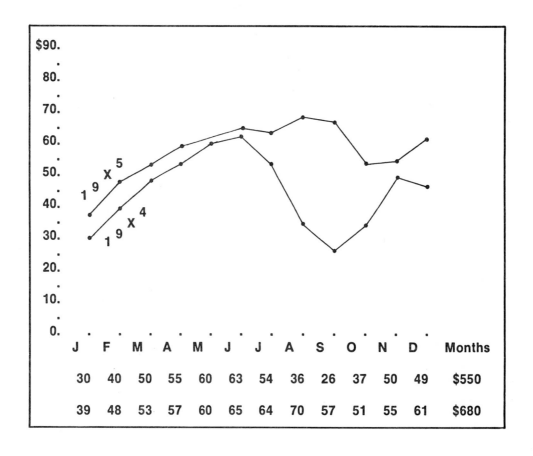

	J	F	M	A	M	J	J	A	S	O	N	D	Months
	30	40	50	55	60	63	54	36	26	37	50	49	$550
	39	48	53	57	60	65	64	70	57	51	55	61	$680

repaid from cash generated by earnings. It is easier to forecast and plan long-range amortization of debt by analyzing prior period trends. Trend lines can be graphed where they have been developed over a satisfactory period of time. This analysis can then be projected forward. The forecast should be compared with results on a routine basis, usually quarterly.

Judgment cannot be overemphasized. A trend line may have occurred during the last two years in billings, receivables, and cash which may change due to major new specific factors. Let us look at the cash account of a public accounting firm grossing $680,000 in 19X5 and $550,000 in 19X4. (See Illustration #5.)

In 19X4 the cash receipts fell to a low in October of $26,000. In October 19X5, the receipts were $57,000 and the fall-off occurred in November to $51,000. The public accounting firm had an increase in collections due to specific causes. Obviously, there had to be new and additional services performed. Most public accounting firms can forecast future receipts based on present and anticipated clients.

The public accounting firm whose receipts are set forth in Illustration #5 had a major tax clientele in 19X4. Certain large new clients whose fiscal years ended in the second calendar quarter added significantly to the cash receipts during the former downturn period. Collections from these new clients can be forecasted. If the public accounting firm had to borrow in 19X4 during the decline, this condition changed in 19X5. The necessity to borrow could be forecast as well as the fact that borrowing would not be needed in October 19X5. Monthly receivable balances can be charted similarly.

Many personal service businesses tend to ignore their receivables because they file their income tax returns on a cash basis. This approach distorts planning and measurement. Receivables and work-in-progress grow as the practice grows. It is a fallacy to assume that receivable balances at the beginning of the period will be the same at the end and that therefore only cash receipts are significant.

Fixed asset acquisitions by professional service organizations arise when the organization is set up, expands, contracts, moves or refurbishes. This is not a monthly or annually recurring event. Balance sheet trends will show little change over extended periods of time.

Professionals usually are conservative and do not like to borrow. It makes very little financial sense to deplete cash balances to purchase fixed assets. You should advise your client to finance fixed assets. Doctors and dentists traditionally finance equipment; so should attorneys, accountants and other professionals. Of course, when your client is opening his own dental office, he must make an investment in the requisite equipment. The legal firm or public accounting firm furnishing a new office should use the same concept as a doctor or dentist. The set-up cost should be paid for out of future related earnings. Long-term financing of these set-up costs is the logical step. Usually bank financing or leasing is available to the professional. Debt service which includes interest and amortization of principal is considered just another cost of doing business. Most professionals also believe that this type of expenditure as it relates to their office is mandatory.

MANAGEMENT SERVICE

Trend analysis may often be performed by a public accounting firm for its clients. This is a fairly simple procedure for public accounting firms to accomplish when financial statements are being typed. Some firms keep a book for each client who desires this type of management service. Once the public accounting firm has initiated and implemented this type of service, the client company should take over this function where feasible.

Your client will appreciate in most instances your presenting him with a series of his balance sheets which you and he can analyze together. It is easiest to begin this with your usual financials. Then the dollar amounts can be translated into percentages.

Many times we find that a new client has prepared no or too few interim balance sheets. In that event, he will see, by comparing many annual balance sheets, that he should be analyzing interim balance sheets. If you are requested to perform these services, it will mean more work for you and a better management information system for your client.

Balance sheet trend analysis is fairly comparable from one service business to another because inventories are only incidental to the total assets of any service business. The major area of difference is in the area of receivables. In some businesses such as bowling alleys and car washes, no credit is usually extended. Therefore, no receivables are generated. In most service businesses, receivables are a major account in the balance sheet.

HOW TO LEVERAGE RECEIVABLES TO MAXIMIZE EARNINGS

The service business may have an operations problem if, in gaining new business, receivables grow too rapidly or if receivables are not collected fast enough. If the service business is undercapitalized, or the collection period lengthens, it may be necessary or advisable to borrow against the receivables to provide the cash necessary to run the operation.

As the accountant for a service business client, it will be your task to evaluate the needs of your client to give him the proper advice and guidance or answer his questions.

You should review or determine the cash needed to run the business. Cash is required to start up a business and run the operation. Where time is a saleable asset, such as in the personal service business, cash needs are less. Where cash is used to acquire fixed assets and these assets are then leased or rented, cash flows must be larger and more significant.

Leveraging of your client's receivables could be important if cash is used to acquire fixed assets. The key question you must determine is, "Does your client have adequate capital and adequate cash?"

Hospitals and Nursing Homes—Today this type of business is reimbursed, usually by some government agency or insurance carrier for its services rendered. Financing of receivables should not be necessary because of the short collection period. More important, patients paying directly should not be discharged to eliminate a receivable problem unless reimbursed by a third party such as an insurance carrier or a government agency.

Hotels and Motels—Most operators are paid when the guest "checks out." Payments not in cash may be financed through the use of credit cards such as American Express, Diners Club, Bank Americard, etc. The credit card company usually pays the charge within several days. Large hotel chains finance their own receivables. Thus, significant amounts of cash are not tied up in receivables.

Leasing Companies—There are two types of leasing companies. The first type owns fixed assets and is in the business of leasing these assets, such as a truck or auto renting company or a company renting tuxedos. The second type is in the finance business, purchasing fixed assets from its customers or for its customers generating leasing receivables. Both types of companies earn money by selling the lease at a price higher than their costs or financing the lease at a lower interest rate than the lease earns. In this business it is essential to turn the receivable and lease back into cash so that the company has funds to begin the next cycle. If you have a leasing company client, you should review its banking arrangements. If you can help this type of client to leverage its receivables, it will be able to acquire additional revenue-producing assets to increase its earnings.

Personal Services—Earnings of clients rendering personal services ordinarily will not be improved by selling or factoring receivables. The growth of this type of business usually is not retarded by a large growth of receivables. If you have a professional client such as an attorney or an architect, you should advise him to collect his receivables faster rather than to try to sell or pledge the receivables with a lending institution.

HOW TO KEEP A TIGHT REIN OVER RECEIVABLES

Receivables are a major asset of nearly all service businesses. The manufacturer, wholesaler or retailer has to contend with inventory turnover rates. The more rapid the turn of inventory, the less that capital is tied up in his business. The service business has no such problem. Receivable control is instead a major factor in minimizing the capital requirements of the business. Keeping a tight rein is paramount.

Two Flash Signals to Watch:

Aging

Each business has its own terms of payment. Usually service businesses require payment within thirty days. Therefore, your client or company should age its receivable schedule every month. Past-due accounts should be monitored continuously. Management should be alerted to the relationships within the aging by watching trends in the percentages as exhibited in Illustration #6.

	ILLUSTRATION #6					
	OCTOBER 31		NOVEMBER 30		DECEMBER 31	
Days	Dollars	Percent	Dollars	Percent	Dollars	Percent
30	$310,000	64.5	$287,000	62.2	$251,000	61.0
60	102,000	21.3	94,000	20.4	83,000	20.1
90	26,000	5.4	35,000	7.7	32,000	7.7
Over 90	42,000	8.8	45,000	9.7	46,000	11.2
TOTALS	$480,000	100.0	$461,000	100.0	$412,000	100.0

In this illustration, the percentage trend analysis clearly shows a heaviness in the older receivables which is not so readily evident in the dollar amounts.

In fact, total receivables actually declined $68,000. Your client may believe that he is doing a better job of collecting, whereas the opposite is true. The receivables are in poorer condition age-wise on December 31 than on October 31. Ninety days and over ninety amounted to 14.2% of total receivables on October 31. This category increased to 18.9% on December 31, or an increase of 4.7%, which represents a change of 33%. Over-ninety-day receivables increased from 8.8% on October 31 to 11.2% on December 31, or a change of 27%. Trend analysis which was discussed at the beginning of this chapter is necessary here.

What should the time frame be? The answer depends upon the kind of service business and its seasonality. Usually a two-year period for trend analysis is most informative. The current year can be compared to the prior year on a month-by-month basis.

Number of Collection Days

Your client should compute the number of collection days of accounts receivable and compare this amount with prior periods using a two-year trend analysis.

For example, if on March 31, 19X6 your client's collection day amount is sixty (60) days and one month later on April 30, 19X6 the amount is fifty (50) days, or a decline of ten (10) days, this would be a positive trend. Of course on a longer time frame, two years, it might look differently as shown in Illustration #7.

ILLUSTRATION #7
NUMBER OF COLLECTION DAYS

	JAN.	FEB.	MAR.	APR.	MAY	JUN.	JUL.	AUG.	SEP.	OCT.	NOV.	DEC.
19X5	54	56	57	31	33	37	43	49	50	51	51	52
19X6	55	60	60	50	53	59	69	72	74	70	67	68

This trend indicates a negative posture. March to April in the prior year dropped approximately 50%, whereas the current March to April decline was only approximately 17%. Your client should find out in May if this is an industry trend or if it is a trend only in his company. If the industry trend is similar, then there is not a great deal he can do to reduce his receivables. If the industry trend is not similar, it is imperative that steps be taken to speed up collections.

As the year progresses we see a slowing down of collections. The analysis and steps taken in May, June, July and August do result in a change in the trend. Collections improved in September and thereafter compared to the fourth-quarter annual period of the prior year when the number of collection days was fairly constant.

The number of collection days at the end of the month is computed first by dividing the sales on open account or credit sales for the month by the number of days in the month. This amount is the "sales per day." The total accounts receivable at month's end is then divided by the "sales per day." The resultant number is "collection days." To illustrate, if April credit sales totalled $60,000, the sales per day would be $2,000 per day. If the balance in the accounts receivable account on April 30, 19X6 was $100,000, then $2,000 per day divided into $100,000 results in 50 collection days.

COLLECTION TECHNIQUES

Keeping a tight rein over receivables should include one or more of the following collection techniques:

a. Advance payments, deposits or retainers before services are rendered.
b. Progress billings during the period services are rendered.
c. Stop services.
    1. Evict tenants.
    2. Obtain a lien on assets in custody.
d. Repossess assets in customer's hands.
e. Obtain evidence of indebtedness such as notes from the recipient of the services. Notes receivable can be used by your service business client in a variety of ways, including a sale of the note or discounting at your client's bank.
f. Use of an independent agency or an attorney to collect.
g. Assess a service charge for late payment.
h. Sue. This procedure usually means that a significant portion of all of the receivables will become uncollectible. Therefore, it should be the last step in the collection process.

HOW TO SPOT UNDERUSED OR UNUSED
ASSETS IN THE BALANCE SHEET

Revenues are generated from either personal services or the utilization of what is normally described as "fixed" assets in a service business. Sometimes a combination of personal service and "fixed" asset service is sold, such as in the operation of bowling alleys, telephone answering services, hospitals, television and radio stations and so on.

Many service businesses acquire unnecessary assets or fail to utilize certain assets. If you are retained by a service-type client, look at the balance sheet and ask yourself:

1. Is each asset needed?
2. Can any asset be turned into cash by
   a. selling it?
   b. selling it and leasing it back?
   c. borrowing against it?
   d. selling it and renting a comparable asset?
   e. selling it and sharing someone else's asset?
3. Is it feasible to share the asset with others?
4. Can the asset be modified or improved to share it with others or to provide more earnings in some other manner?

Certain categories of assets tend to be underused. If your client is providing a personal service, look first at the fixed asset accounts such as furniture, fixtures and equipment. Then look at the fixed assets themselves. Observe the organization of work in your client's office. Some companies provide certain fixed assets to their employees as "fringe benefits" such as a company car. If this is your client's policy, you can help unfreeze needed cash by suggesting that the car or cars be leased rather than owned.

Attitudes and goals are important. Many successful clients may defend underutilization of assets by saying, "This is how we have always done it."

We reply, "Times are changing. Old policies or procedures should be reevaluated. If it made sense twenty years ago it probably doesn't make sense now."

Beware of the cash-rich client. He may need assets into which he can lock up his surplus monies. Under present income tax laws, a successful corporation must reinvest in its business, declare dividends or be taxed on "unreasonable accumulation of earnings" by the Federal government. Therefore, a car fleet can be owned rather than leased by your client in order to avoid taxes. A real estate corporation may overpay for additional real estate rather than declare dividends or be subject to the tax on "unreasonable accumulation of earnings."

LONG-RANGE BALANCE SHEET PLANNING

To provide this type of service for your client, you must know your client and your client's goals. Where is he going? What will he need to get there? Long-range balance sheet planning is really asset-liability management strategy.

Many times we have asked a new client what his goals are only to find out that he had not clearly defined them himself. Recently one young president of a corporation answered that question by saying:

To retire in eight years.

Sitting in an accountant's office, a doctor or dentist might reply:

To stop paying income taxes.

Obviously these goals are not in the purview of long-range balance sheet planning. Your client, if you are a public accountant, or your company, if you are a private accountant, should have a goal or goals which can be quantified into a written business plan or professional plan. The key word is "plan." Each service business demands a very different type of plan. Timing is also essential. If you have a client who is planning to acquire a radio station, the balance sheet strategy is very different than the strategy for the client who is presently operating a radio station. If your client is about to buy a piece of real estate, say a shopping center, the planning required is different than if he is going to erect one or if he is operating one.

Look back to Illustration #2 shown on page 60 of this chapter. Using time-series analysis, this company was reevaluating its long-range balance sheet planning. It was building up more cash than it needed in its operations and was holding onto it. This company looked at the alternative uses of its cash: More assets, larger dividends or some other strategy?

Many companies are organized and can grow without a written business plan. The original plan is in the mind of the original entrepreneur. As the company grows and time passes, the plan is followed, modified or possibly improved. Too often no new course is charted, the plan grows stale and new competition comes in with better plans and ideas. The company can die or be sold or merged out of existence.

When aviation was in its infancy, the pilots flew pretty much by the seat of their pants. They instinctively knew how to react and control their planes. Many businessmen run their businesses the same way. As planes and flying became more complex, pilots had to rely on instruments and plans. Every time a pilot took off, he had to file a flight plan. Many of the old-time pilots died trying to fly by the seat of their pants. What they had learned was no longer relevant.

If your client is unable to put his business plan in writing, this is another opportunity to be of service. You should help him quantify his needs. Ask him all the key questions and see if his answers make sense to you. What is his forecasted cash need, month by month, for the next year, two years, three years? Why?

If you are unfamiliar with the business your client is in or plans to go into, you can usually obtain balance sheet and other financial data from trade organizations or services such as Dun & Bradstreet or the Robert Morris Associates, which compile such statistics.

KEY QUESTIONS TO ASK IN TAILORING A LONG-RANGE BALANCE SHEET PLAN

Let's take a new client and set up a long-range balance sheet plan. The key questions you should ask are:

1. What are the goals?
2. What assets will be acquired at what cost?
3. What funds are available to acquire these assets?
4. If financing is needed, what are the alternatives?
5. If financing is needed, how much cash will be realized from the operations to satisfy the debt?
6. Will the operation generate enough cash to pay your client an amount necessary for him to live as he requires or will he have to live on less during the start-up phase and possibly longer?
7. How much is needed in the way of start-up cash after the operation has begun but before receivables are collected? To answer this question, you should have your client forecast week by week for at least one year all operating costs such as payroll and related fringe costs, rent and all other overhead. You will probably have to supply him with the various tax costs, for example, payroll taxes, personal property taxes, franchise taxes, real estate taxes, income taxes, etc., and the timetable for payment.
8. What is the contingency plan in the event that the actual operations do not produce the desired results? For example, operations may not generate adequate revenues. Costs may be higher than anticipated.
9. Try to get your client to forecast what his balance sheet will look like one year from the day he begins operating.
10. Finally, you should be sure that the plan is monitored, updated and revised at least monthly, especially if this is a new business.

3

Cash Flow—How to Show Clients Where the Money Is Coming from and Going to

HOW TO PREPARE THE STATEMENT OF CHANGES IN FINANCIAL POSITION

You should prepare a statement of changes in financial position which should start with "cash" at the beginning and not "working capital." In APB Opinion #19 issued in 1971, there is set forth a mandate to the accounting profession:

> . . . a working capital format is not relevant to an entity that does not distinguish between current and non-current assets and liabilities . . .

The clearest explanation of changes in financial position is the change in "cash" from the beginning of the period to the end of the period. This analysis is preferable to demonstrate how the operation of the business generated the cash needed for future operations. Excesses or shortages of cash generated are set forth for analysis.

Some of your service business clients may prefer another approach which we shall call the "all-asset" approach. In this presentation, the statement of changes in financial position begins with "total assets" and ends with "total assets." The change in "total assets" is analyzed instead of "cash."

REQUIREMENTS OF APB OPINION #19

In the preparation of the statement of changes in financial position, APB Opinion #19 requires that the effect of financing and investing by your client be disclosed in the following areas:

1. Asset acquisition—long-life assets only, such as:
   a. Property
   b. Investments
   c. Intangibles
2. Asset sales of long-life assets not in the normal course of business
3. Conversion of debt or preferred stock to common
4. Long-term debt transactions including:
   a. Issuance
   b. Repayment
   c. Assumption
   d. Redemption
5. Issuance of capital stock or asset exchange for stock
6. Cash or other dividend distributions

The flow of cash through a service business may be analyzed by analyzing the statement of changes in cash position. The statement may be in balance form or in a form expressing changes in cash. Most service businesses should employ the latter form. Let's look at the forms in Illustrations #1 and #2.

ILLUSTRATION #1

TRUCK LEASING CORP.

STATEMENT OF CHANGES IN CASH POSITION

FOR THE YEAR ENDED DECEMBER 31, 19XX

CASH—BEGINNING .... $ 34,000

ADD:

  SOURCES OF CASH

Net income		$ 45,000	
Items not requiring the use of cash			
Depreciation		20,000	
Accounts payable—increase	$ 12,000		
Income taxes payable—increase	6,000		
Taxes and expenses accrued—			
increase	10,000		
Bank financing	74,000		
		102,000	
TOTAL CASH PROVIDED		$ 167,000	

DEDUCT:

  USES OF CASH

Investment in trucks	$ 61,000		
Loans receivables—increase	77,000		
Inventory—increase	20,000		
Deposit and other assets—increase	4,000		
TOTAL CASH USED		162,000	

INCREASE IN CASH   5,000

CASH—ENDING .... $ 39,000

ILLUSTRATION #2

REALTY OPERATING CO., INC.

STATEMENT OF CHANGES IN FINANCIAL POSITION

FOR THE YEARS ENDED JUNE 30, 19X8

	19X8	19X7
SOURCES OF CASH:		
Net income	$ 6,270	$ 5,720
Items not providing or requiring the use of cash:		
Depreciation of real estate and amortization of tenant alterations and leasing and financing costs	10,360	9,180
Deferred income taxes	3,100	4,110
Excess of cash provided from disposition of real estate over amount of profit— net	3,780	1,000
Other—net, principally changes in accounts receivable and accounts payable	6,600	(1,610)
CASH PROVIDED BY OPERATIONS	$30,110	$18,400
Mortgage loans and other financing	69,700	57,900
	$99,810	$76,300
USES OF CASH:		
Cash dividends	$ 2,410	$ 2,300
Expenditures for construction and acquisition of real estate and equipment	76,200	58,760
Expenditures for alterations, leasing and other deferred items	8,250	9,300
Payments in reduction of mortgages payable and notes payable	5,860	4,100
Other—net, principally changes in accounts receivable and accounts payable relating to capital expenditures	4,650	(280)
	$97,370	$74,180
INCREASE IN CASH	$ 2,440	$ 2,120
	$99,810	$76,300

HOW NOT TO PREPARE THE STATEMENT OF CHANGES IN FINANCIAL POSITION

Illustration #3 on page 82 is a good example of how not to prepare a statement of changes in financial position because it is based on the concept of working capital.

During the year ended December 31, 19X2, the company had earnings of $1,791,000, yet it had a working capital decrease of $1,820,000. At the next year-end, December 31, 19X3, the company lost $874,000. However, the working capital that year only declined $1,028,000. In both years, according to this illustration, the working capital provided from operations was approximately $4,200,000. In other words, although the company was provided $1,791,000 of funds from earnings in 19X2 and used for its loss in 19X3 the sum of $874,000, a shift of $2,665,000, the working capital increased approximately $4,200,000 each year before it applied its funds to arrive at a decrease in working capital. Obviously, this analysis of changes in working capital is misleading. It would seem likely that when this company was successful the working capital declined even more than when it was unprofitable. The reader who sees the company move in this direction would tend to believe that the company's position was deteriorating rather than improving. Therefore, this format is not recommended for this statement.

HOW YOUR CLIENT SHOULD USE THE STATEMENT OF CHANGES IN FINANCIAL POSITION (CASH POSITION)

The first step is to prepare a forecast to ascertain what will happen to the business by simulating a set of balance sheet models.

Using the historical past as a guide, obtain an estimate from management as to the assets to be employed in the future. A series of balance sheets should be prepared on a *pro forma* basis giving effect to anticipated needs and uses on an interim basis and at the end of the next fiscal year. Some companies will need this type of forecast for more than one year.

ILLUSTRATION #3
DREDGE & DOCK COMPANY
STATEMENT OF CHANGES IN FINANCIAL POSITION
FOR THE YEARS ENDED DECEMBER 31, 19X3

	19X3	19X2
	(In thousands)	
SOURCE OF WORKING CAPITAL		
Operations		
Net earnings (loss)	$ (874)	$ 1,791
Add: Charges (deduct credits) not affecting working capital:		
Depreciation	3,548	3,684
Deferred federal income tax	1,488	(1,275)
WORKING CAPITAL PROVIDED FROM OPERATIONS	$ 4,162	$ 4,200
Sale and retirement of plant and equipment	73	304
Reduction of advances and other receivables	193	—
	$ 4,428	$ 4,504
APPLICATION OF WORKING CAPITAL:		
Dividends	$ 1,266	$ 1,583
Expenditures for plant and equipment	4,190	4,319
Increase in advances and other receivables	—	422
	$ 5,456	$ 6,324
(DECREASE) IN WORKING CAPITAL	$(1,028)	$(1,820)
CHANGES IN WORKING CAPITAL		
INCREASE (DECREASE) IN CURRENT ASSETS		
Cash	$ 703	$ (850)
Marketable securities	(935)	(4,445)
Accounts receivable	2,665	1,627
Costs and estimated earnings in excess of billings	(3,084)	2,340
Inventories and prepaid expenses	1,488	260
	$ 837	$(1,068)
INCREASE (DECREASE) IN CURRENT LIABILITIES		
Accounts payable and accrued expenses	$ (202)	$ 1,178
Billings in excess of costs and estimated earnings	2,576	223
Taxes on income and other	(509)	(649)
	$ 1,865	$ 752
(DECREASE) IN WORKING CAPITAL	$(1,028)	$(1,820)

As an example, a company in the truck leasing business will have to project its monthly truck acquisitions to arrive at a total fixed-asset picture for each future balance sheet. Retirements should be planned to obtain the complete truck position. It is much simpler to do this if the company has been in business for some time and historical data are available, especially if the business is seasonal. Once you have made an estimate of asset needs, you can prepare or have the client prepare the asset side of the balance sheet.

Projecting your client's asset needs is not a simple task. However, it is an essential part of the management planning process. Some clients may say, "How do we know what we will need?" We say, "You may not *know* but you should have a good idea, which is all we need to begin to plan. The initial forecast will probably have to be revised anyway."

You may have to explain to your client that the assets required to operate his business must be generated from earnings or borrowings or from an additional infusion of capital. If he has no idea of what he will need, he may run short of cash even though he may be able to operate profitably. Earnings alone may not generate adequate cash to acquire all of the assets needed. Even if he says he could obtain credit from a bank to finance his truck acquisitions, the bank will want to know how much he will want to borrow. Each asset category then should be analyzed in a similar manner, including Trade Receivables, Inventory of Parts and Supplies (if any), Prepaid Assets, Deposits, Other Fixed Assets, and so on. Each asset category can be evaluated using some rational approach. The following are a few suggestions.

UTILIZE PAST HISTORICAL RELATIONSHIPS

The simplest approach to utilizing past historical relationships is to take a series of balance sheets at the end of the fiscal year and determine the changes in each asset category, then convert the dollar amounts into percentages.

For example, if assets total $175,000, convert the total into 100%, and each asset category should be converted in dollar number into a percentage of the total. Then take the current fiscal year-end balance sheet and project one year in advance using the percentage changes which you have determined from the historical past. Each asset category should be analyzed in order to prepare the forecast. Look at Illustration #4 of Truck Leasing Corp. These receivables, for example, have been increasing between 20% and 25% each year. Therefore, the projection for the next fiscal year is an increase of 22.6%. In this case the fiscal year began with $252,000 of Lease Receivables. The increase of 22.6% therefore was in the amount of $57,000. Similarly, revenue-producing assets can be forecast to increase 32.6%, which amounts to an increase of $61,000 from the beginning of the fiscal year. When the *pro forma* column is completed, each item should be reviewed by management for reasonableness. In the case of revenue-producing assets, they should be checked against your client's projected acquisitions for the year, from which should be deducted retirements which are planned or estimated. The sum of $61,000, which we have arrived at using a historical basis, can be measured against your client's "Guesstimate" or forecast.

ILLUSTRATION #4

TRUCK LEASING CORP.

BALANCE SHEET

ASSETS	BEGINNING FISCAL YEAR	PRO FORMA END OF FISCAL YEAR	DIFFERENCE
Cash	$ 34,000	$ 39,000	$ 5,000
Lease receivables (gross of allowance for doubtful accounts)	252,000	309,000	57,000
Inventory—parts—at cost ..	71,000	91,000	20,000
Revenue-producing assets —at cost	187,000	248,000	61,000
Deposit and other assets	58,000	62,000	4,000
TOTAL ASSETS	$602,000	$749,000	$147,000

In this illustration, the total increase in assets of $147,000 is an increase of 24.4% from the beginning of the fiscal year to the end. This total percentage increase should also be relevant. In other words, if you find in preparing your projections that the increase has been averaging between 25% and 35% for the total assets, obviously a 24.4% increase which you are now projecting does not measure up to the historical past. Therefore, all of the numbers should be revised so that the total asset projection falls in line with the historical past. At this point, your client may disagree with your forecast because there may be some change in the economy, the business mix or some other factor which should be taken into account, thereby raising or lowering the percentage change of total assets.

USE ANNUAL STATEMENTS STUDIES

Annually the Robert Morris Associates prepare a statistical study for most industries. If your client is not satisfied with the historical approach, does not have an adequate history, or is starting a new business, you may want to prepare your *pro forma* based on the percentages developed annually by the Robert Morris Associates. Again, if you use the balance sheet information prepared in the studies, the *pro forma* information which you developed should be analyzed by management to see that the information you are projecting is relevant.

There are many other sources from which to prepare the information, such as Dun and Bradstreet and other information-gathering agencies. Many industries have trade groups or associations which annually analyze the industry and prepare detailed financial studies. Finally, there are many public accounting firms that specialize in certain types of businesses, some of which gather industry data or are familiar with trends in that particular industry.

At this point you will have enough data to prepare the asset side of a *pro forma* balance sheet at fiscal year end. The increase in "total assets" other than cash will have to be sustained from:

a. Earnings
b. Borrowing

 c. Additional capital infusion
 d. Leasing of assets
 e. Any combination of the above

In Illustration #4, total assets increased in the amount of $147,000. Where will the funds come from to provide for this increase (including the increase in cash)? To answer the question it will be necessary to do two things:

 1. Prepare the liability side of the *pro forma* balance sheet.
 2. Forecast earnings.

HOW TO GO ABOUT PREPARING THE LIABILITY SIDE

It is important to forecast the increase in total liabilities in order to ascertain whether this amount is adequate to sustain the increase in assets which you have just forecast. Usually this increase is inadequate and the balance of funds required will come from earnings, additional capital infusion or some adjustment of the assets, possibly a lease of certain other acquired assets rather than a direct asset purchase.

The approach to the preparation of the liability side of the *pro forma* balance sheet is similar to the approach in the preparation of the asset side. The best way to begin is, again, to review the historical past and to ascertain the changes in the composition of the various liabilities. If your client/company is going into a new business or does not have an adequate historical relationship from which to project, again, there are many sources, such as the Robert Morris Associates, Dun and Bradstreet or trade organizations which prepare financial studies annually. Each liability should be forecast.

Let us look at Truck Leasing Corp., Illustration #5.

ILLUSTRATION #5

TRUCK LEASING CORP.

BALANCE SHEET

LIABILITIES	BEGINNING OF FISCAL YEAR	*PRO FORMA* END OF FISCAL YEAR	DIFFERENCE
Notes payable—bank (Due within one year—$67,000 beginning; $83,000 ending)	$297,000	$371,000	$ 74,000
Accounts payable	43,000	55,000	12,000
Income taxes payable	8,000	14,000	6,000
Taxes and expenses accrued	44,000	54,000	10,000
TOTAL LIABILITIES	$392,000	$494,000	$102,000
STOCKHOLDERS' EQUITY			
Capital stock	$ 65,000	$ 65,000	$ —
Retained earnings	145,000	190,000	45,000
TOTAL STOCKHOLDERS' EQUITY	$210,000	$255,000	$ 45,000
TOTAL LIABILITIES AND STOCKHOLDERS' EQUITY	$602,000	$749,000	$147,000

PROJECTING EARNINGS

The task of projecting earnings a full year in advance is probably the most difficult task. If your client has been in business for some time, one approach is to use the return on stockholders' equity. If your client has been averaging a return on opening stockholders' equity of approximately 20%, then it is conceivable that if your client is Trucking Leasing Corp., in the previous illustration, he could earn anywhere from $40,000 to $45,000 in the ensuing year. You should take into account internal as as well as external factors. Furthermore, be cautious. It is better to understate an earnings forecast in order to determine that additional financing will be necessary then to overstate earnings and fall short of the cash necessary to finance the increase in assets. Internally, your client should arrive at his own projection based on his anticipated sales for the next year and his anticipated cost of doing business. Externally, you and/or your client should evaluate such factors as economic forecasting for the next year for the entire country or specific forecasts for your client's industry. Many economists working for the federal government prepare economic forecasts, and there are many other sources available such as financial institutions where economists render their opinion, as well as trade associations and companies that specifically perform this function for large corporations.

By preparing the asset and liability sides of the balance sheet on a *pro forma* basis you automatically come up with the change in stockholders' equity. Illustration #5 of the Truck Leasing Corp. shows a change in retained earnings of $45,000, which is a forecast of earnings for the coming fiscal year. This sum should agree with the conservative forecast by your client. If it does not, it is safer to use your client's own forecast than to revise the liability side of the *pro forma* balance sheet.

CASH SHORTAGES

Although there is a forecasted increase of total liabilities in the amount of $102,000 in Illustration #5, the forecast assumes that bank borrowings will increase in the amount of $74,000. In other words, it will be necessary to increase bank lines of credit in order to be able to borrow an additional $74,000 during the fiscal year. The alternative to obtaining this additional financing would be to restrict asset acquisitions or to sell off certain assets such as receivables generated from leasing assets.

There are a number of other financing options open in the event that the bank is unwilling to increase its lines. For example, your client might be eligible for a loan from the Small Business Administration (SBA) or your client might approach another financial institution such as an insurance company. Finally, additional cash might be invested into the corporation, or other investors can be brought in.

THE SURPRISE THEORY

One major advantage of producing a *pro forma* balance sheet is to eliminate the element of surprise. **Illustration:** If your client did not provide himself additional bank or other sources of funds to obtain $74,000 needed, he would then be in the position at the end of the fiscal year where he would have earned a very satisfactory return on his investment but would find himself short of cash. The $39,000 that was forecasted in the *pro forma* balance sheet at the end of the fiscal year would have been used to finance the $74,000 required for additional bank loans, and there would be a deficit in the amount of $35,000. A successful business cannot operate with this type of surprise.

At this point it would be wise to review all operating policies to determine if the flow of cash can be improved:

a. by changing the terms of sale in order to obtain more cash and reduce the amount of the receivable required to be held by your client.
b. by entering into proper financing arrangements for each of the truck acquisitions so that the amounts your client will have to pay for each of the trucks will be exceeded by the cash flow from the receivables generated from the customers.

    c. by selling the receivables to financing companies, generating enough cash to pay the liability.

Whatever step is taken to improve cash flow, it must be evaluated to determine its impact not only on the balance sheet but also on the income statement. For example, if your client decides to raise funds by selling his receivables, he may have to do so at a discount which would then impair his earnings, creating additional cash shortages which must be qualified on a *pro forma* basis.

It is important to recognize that there are peaks and valleys of cash flow during the fiscal year. Though your forecast may be a good one on an annual basis, on a short-run basis there may be temporary periods where additional bank lines or other financing may be requried. For example, income taxes are paid quarterly in advance. When these payments are made, large amounts of cash may be necessary. Therefore, it is usually a good idea to prepare this *pro forma* on an interim basis, either monthly or weekly, in order to pinpoint the dates during the year when cash shortages will occur as well as when there will be excess cash available. Sometimes a simpler expedient may be used by your client to husband cash. For example, if your client has a large payroll and he pays weekly, he may find that his cash flow will be beneficial if he can change to a bi-monthly payroll. Of course, other factors beyond his control may prevent this, such as union contract requirements.

HOW TO SEE WHAT IS HAPPENING TO THE CASH IN THE BUSINESS

Every service businessman is interested in finding out what has been happening to his cash. Also, he will need to know what will happen. There are two approaches to this problem: a) historical and b) future or *pro forma*.

HISTORICAL CASH FLOW

If your client prepares a statement of changes in cash position each month, he will be able to see what has happened to the cash in the business. This financial statement should be prepared for the month and cumulatively from the beginning of the fiscal year to date.

It is important that you meet with your client to review the statement of changes in cash position if he has not used this tool in order to analyze the reasons for the changes in each of the asset and liability categories. Client education is an important factor because if you do not explain this statement to your client, he may not understand it and may not be able to use it effectively.

Another approach to see what has happened to the cash in the business is to prepare a series of monthly balance sheets that indicate in another column the difference for each account between the beginning and ending of the month or period. This type of approach is similar to trend analysis, which we have discussed in Chapter 2.

The accounts in the balance sheet are listed in a vertical column. On the left-hand side of each column is the account balance at the end of the last fiscal year. In the first right-hand column is the balance at the end of the first month of the new fiscal year. In the second column is the monthly change or the difference from the end of the fiscal year to the end of the first month after the fiscal year. In the third column is the second month of the fiscal year. In the fourth column is the monthly change between the end of the first month and the second month. In the next column is the cumulative difference between the end of the last fiscal year and the end of the second month. This continues for at least an eight- to twelve-month time frame as shown in Illustration #6 entitled, "Balance Sheet Trend Analysis," shown on page 92.

FUTURE CASH FLOW NEEDS

Another important task that you should perform for your client is to forecast future cash flow needs. For example, if long-term debt financing has been arranged and this debt is being amortized monthly or quarterly, it is very valuable to compare the cash flow with the amount needed to service the amortization of this debt. Here again, you must project net income plus de-

ILLUSTRATION #6

BALANCE SHEET TREND ANALYSIS

December	January	Monthly Change	February	Monthly Change	Cum. Change	March	Monthly Change	Cum. Change
$ 34,000 Cash	$ 42,000	$ 8,000	$ 9,000	$ (33,000)	$ (25,000)	$ 35,900	$ 26,900	$ 1,900
252,000 Lease receivables	254,500	2,500	256,100	1,600	4,100	247,200	(8,900)	(4,800)
187,000 Revenue-producing assets	196,000	9,000	207,100	11,100	20,100	203,000	(4,100)	16,000

92

preciation on a monthly basis in order to relate the cash flows that are generated to the debt service required.

HOW TO RECOGNIZE CASH PROBLEMS BEFORE THEY OCCUR

Many companies try to recognize cash problems before they occur by preparing an annual cash budget. Usually this budget is a monthly forecast. Each month, receipts of cash from all sources are projected and totalled. Then all uses of cash are projected for the month. The difference becomes the cash excess or deficiency for the month. Cumulatively, the cash excess or deficiency is computed.

After this budget is prepared, the cash deficiency periods are anticipated by arranging for borrowing from a bank or other financial institution or by making some arrangement with creditors such as changing terms. For example, some companies will issue notes to their creditors in order to overcome deficiences in one period. These notes are set so that they can be paid when there is an excess of cash forecast.

After the annual cash budget is prepared, the monthly projection should be compared with actual results in order to anticipate future problems.

This process of comparison should cause the annual cash budget to be revised after comparison with the actual monthly results. If, for example, receipts from collections of receivables have been budgeted in the amount of $25,000 for the month of January and the amount is actually $22,000, it is important to review the reasons therefore. You may find out that anticipated January receipts will be forthcoming in the month of February, and therefore, the February forecast of $35,000 will be closer to $38,000 when the month is closed out. On the other hand, the reason for the reduction from $25,000 to $22,000 in January may be a slowness in all accounts. Therefore, it may be wise to reduce the annual budget for all future months since the collection rate has slowed down.

Here is a signal that the cash problem will occur. The question is, "What can be done?" The solutions depend upon the nature of your client's business and the economic climate at the time of the problem.

Don't let anyone tell you that he is unable to prepare an annual cash budget because he cannot forecast when he will receive cash from his collection of receivables. Tell him that if he does not receive the cash in one month, he will surely receive it in the next month, and if he uses the historical approach to evaluate his receipts he will come up with a reasonable approximation. Certainly you can tell him that he can forecast fairly accurately how he is going to spend his cash and in what time frame. Here again, client education is important, because if he fails to prepare an annual cash budget, he may be surprised that he may run short of cash even though his business is being run on a very profitable basis and he is generating substantial earnings. This is especially true of a successful business.

You can be very helpful to your client throughout this entire process by reviewing the terms of his sales and the terms of his trade credit in order to control the cash flow to prevent cash deficiencies.

Usually at the end of the quarter, but certainly no later than the six-month period after preparing an annual cash budget and comparing the actual with the *pro forma*, it is recommended that the *pro forma* be revised based on experience to date. Furthermore, as business conditions change it is necessary to take these changes into account, such as the slowing down of cash receipts from receivables which occurs in times of business recessions. Cash outflows will probably be monitored continously throughout the month.

One important point to bear in mind in connection with an annual cash budget is that all disbursements must be forecast, including purchases of fixed assets, payment of bank debt, income tax payments, dividends, if any, and other items which normally would not fall into an operating expense type budget.

Finally, it is important to prepare this budget in order to determine the minimum balance of cash that the company should plan to have on hand to maintain as a buffer against the danger that cash outflows will be higher or cash inflows lower than anticipated. Of course if the company has adequate bank lines arranged and can obtain additional short-term funds readily, then the acceptable balance of cash may be reduced.

Let us look at a semi-annual budget as shown in Illustration #7.

ILLUSTRATION #7

TRUCK LEASING CORP.

SEMI-ANNUAL CASH BUDGET

	JAN.	FEB.	MAR.	APR.	MAY	JUN.	TOTALS
Cash—beginning	$ 34,000	$ 42,000	$ 9,000	$ 35,900	$ 24,800	$ 18,600	$ 34,000
Cash Receipts							
Collections of accounts receivable	$ 38,300	$ 41,000	$ 57,900	$ 42,200	$ 44,900	$ 51,300	$275,600
Proceeds from truck sales	—	2,900	5,800	—	1,500	2,900	13,100
TOTAL CASH RECEIPTS	$ 38,300	$ 43,900	$ 63,700	$ 42,200	$ 46,400	$ 54,200	$288,700
Cash Payments							
Trucks	$ 9,800	$ 14,900	$ 2,500	$ 33,100	$ 8,900	$ 6,200	$ 75,400
Salaries	9,100	24,900	9,400	9,100	9,800	10,900	73,200
Parts	400	900	1,000	300	2,100	1,200	5,900
Insurance	—	2,700	—	2,700	—	—	5,400
Telephone	200	200	300	200	200	300	1,400
Rent	1,000	1,000	1,000	1,000	1,000	1,000	6,000
Light and power	200	200	200	100	100	100	900
Fuel	1,000	1,000	—	—	—	—	2,000

95

ILLUSTRATION #7 (continued)

TRUCK LEASING CORP.

SEMI-ANNUAL CASH BUDGET

	JAN.	FEB.	MAR.	APR.	MAY	JUN.	TOTALS
Office supplies	—	400	—	300	1,000	600	2,300
Data processing expense	400	400	400	400	500	500	2,600
Promotion	1,500	400	1,200	1,700	700	1,200	6,700
Advertising	200	200	200	300	300	300	1,500
Professional fees	3,000	—	—	1,000	—	—	4,000
Payroll taxes	800	2,100	800	800	800	900	6,200
Union benefits	300	300	300	300	300	300	1,800
Income taxes	—	—	17,500	—	—	8,500	26,000
Debt service							
Interest	2,400	2,300	2,000	2,000	1,900	1,800	12,400
Amortization	—	25,000	—	—	25,000	—	50,000
TOTAL CASH PAYMENTS	$ 30,300	$ 76,900	$ 36,800	$ 53,300	$ 52,600	$ 33,800	$283,700
CASH ENDING	$ 42,000	$ 9,000	$ 35,900	$ 24,800	$ 18,600	$ 39,000	$ 39,000

This budget represents a cash plan for the six months ending June 30. The corporation anticipates total cash receipts or inflows of $288,700, of which $275,600 is from collections of accounts receivable and $13,100 of proceeds from truck sales. These truck sales are trucks which have been out on lease and which are no longer being leased. During this period the company plans to acquire trucks in the amount of $75,400 in accordance with the schedule projected in Illustration #7.

Based on the plan, the corporation at the end of February will have a cash balance in the bank of $9,000. If management believes that this amount is at too low a level, then steps should be taken to adjust the budget. For example, during February the corporation expects to pay $14,900 for trucks to be acquired. If the corporation desires to have a larger balance at the end of February, this $14,900 could be scaled down so that larger truck payments would be made in the month of March, when only $2,500 is forecast for truck payments. By reducing the February payments from $14,900 to $4,900, the February ending balance of cash on hand increases from $9,000 to $19,000. The March payments for trucks would then have to be increased from $2,500 to $12,500.

The corporation at the end of the six-month period expects to amortize $50,000 of its bank debt without incurring any further indebtedness in connection with the acquisition of trucks. This illustrates that the cash flow is adequate for debt service, for all expenses and costs, as well as for expenditures for revenue-producing assets. Obviously, arrangements should be made with a financial institution in the event that the corporation acquires new customers requiring an abnormal unforeseen cash outlay for trucks. This type of arrangement is in the nature of a standby arrangement inasmuch as the semi-annual cash budget shown in Illustration #7 indicates that the cash flow will be adequate to finance the company's operations. Additional financing is not needed during this semi-annual period.

In Illustration #7 there are no dividend payments forecast because, in small privately owned companies, this is the most expensive way to obtain funds from the corporation for its stockholders. Furthermore, a growing privately owned company usually needs to retain its cash for reinvestment into the business. In this instance, cash will be needed to acquire new trucks and to finance lease receivables.

HOW TO CONTROL AND PLAN CASH FLOWS USING REPLACEMENT FUND TECHNIQUES

Funding

Some service businesses lend themselves to replacement fund techniques. For example, in the operation of real estate, well-managed real estate companies usually estimate that a certain percentage of the rent collected should be set aside and deposited into a special cash account, sometimes a savings account, in order to create a replacement fund.

The dollar amount of the replacement fund may be shown as an expense for accounting purposes in the financial statement. Then, at the end of some time frame such as the month or quarter, the budgeted cash amount is withdrawn from the regular cash account and is deposited into a separate replacement fund cash account. For example, if a rent roll is $10,000 a month or $30,000 a quarter, then possibly 2% is set up as a replacement fund, or $600 a quarter. Each quarter, this sum of $600 would be deducted from the general cash account and deposited or segregated into a replacement fund cash account.

The idea behind this replacement fund technique is to plan for future cash needs by setting aside a certain amount previously determined. A small sum deposited continously over a long time usually accumulates and is available for replacement of substantial fixed assets.

Certain governmental agencies such as the Federal Housing Administration (FHA), in connection with mortgage financing insured by the FHA, actually require the use of a replacement fund technique such as the one described.

Matching

If your client owns a radio station or a television station, this would be a good device to utilize for replacement of certain assets which may last only two, three or four years. The cost of replacement may recreate a hardship at that time, unless the replacement fund technique is employed. Most service businesses plan cash flow by attempting to match amortization of financing with depreciation. In other words if your client is in the truck leasing business and depreciates each truck over an estimated useful life of three years, then the truck should be financed at least over that three-year period. Of course, if your client can obtain a longer period of financing then the depreciation flow should exceed the amortization requirement.

If your client is involved in a personal service business, here again, the depreciation period should match the amortization of the financing required for the fixed asset. Most personal service businesses require that the cash be accumulated in the business in order that additional funds be available for such purposes as distributing bonuses to personnel and cash distributions to partners after the end of the fiscal year.

Most professional organizations will not allow their partners to withdraw in cash all of the profits at the end of the fiscal year, but require some retention of the earnings in order to control the cash flow. This retention policy for professional service businesses is usually based on an annual cash budget to determine cash requirements. It is also related to standby bank arrangements during periods where receivables are projected to be abnormally large. If substantial fixed assets are required by personal service companies, such as a law firm or CPA firm, it is usually easier in terms of cash flow to borrow the amount needed and repay from future cash flows. Of course the depreciation should match the amortization of the amount to be financed. The more conservative approach is to take the total debt service requirements, including interest and amortization, and match these against the estimated depreciation in terms of time frame.

If, for example, a $36,000 mini-computer is purchased and it is depreciated on a straight-line basis over a four-year estimated useful life at $9,000 a year, obviously a financial institution will loan no more than $36,000. Interest must be paid on the $36,000 over this same four-year time frame. Therefore, your client must be prepared to earn an adequate sum in excess of depreciation which would pay the requisite interest over the four-year term. If the financial institution is willing to make the loan in excess of four years, he may have total interest and amortization expenses of $9,000 a year. But at the end of the fourth year he will still owe money on the remaining balance of the loan depending upon the interest rate during this four-year period. There will be amortization payments to make against which there will be no depreciation charges after the fourth year.

Of course, it is hoped that he will have earnings to match against amortization to be paid after the end of the fourth year. In this case, during the fifth year there will be no depreciation expenses, but amortization as well as interest payments will be required.

In most service companies, the reverse would be true. The fixed asset to be financed will probably require a shorter amortization period than the estimated useful life of the asset. Therefore, depreciation expense will continue after amortization payments are completed.

Fortunately, in most personal service businesses the fixed assets do not play a major role and are not a major cost element. However, the cash flow must be monitored and projected here, too, in order not to run short of cash.

TO SUM UP

Let's go back and recapitulate what cash flow is all about. The essential purpose is to show your client where the money is coming from and going to. To do this, you must prepare and go over the statement of changes in financial position (cash position) with the client. Be sure that you do not fall into the working capital format trap.

After your client has learned how to use this statement, it will be up to you to create a forecast or cash flow. The key to this service is to develop your client's asset needs on a month-to-month basis for at least one year in advance. Then you must forecast the sources of cash which must come from:

    a. Net Income
    b. Depreciation
    c. Financing
    d. Additional Equity

All of this requires persistence and imagination, but you will have the satisfaction of seeing your client operate in a more organized and professional manner.

4

Real Estate—Buy or Lease—Financial Effects on the Business

WHY A SERVICE BUSINESS LOOKS WEAKER WHEN IT OWNS ITS OWN REAL ESTATE AND WHAT TO DO ABOUT IT

Many successful service business companies after a period of time accumulate the funds necessary to acquire the real estate in which they are operating. If they see their geographic area improving or at least stable real-estate-wise, and if their rented property lends itself to an expansion of the business, the successful company may decide to buy the rental property. At this point in time an earnings forecast must be made comparing rental vs. ownership. You should advise your client that he should finance his acquisition with a long-term debt, usually a first mortgage, multiple mortgages or a purchase money-type mortgage. All of the costs of ownership should be obtained and operational costs projected, including the cost of debt service. The key question that must be answered is, "Will the out-of-pocket costs be less if the real estate is owned rather than rented?" If you can answer "yes" to your client, you should next review the income tax consequences of ownership.

After the forecast is prepared and the company concludes that it is more profitable to own than to rent, many service businesses purchase their own real estate. Immediately the financial posture of the company appears to weaken, as illustrated by comparing the following balance sheets in Illustrations #1 and #2.

This company purchased land and building at a total cost of $294,000. It used up $20,000 of its cash, and the seller repaid its security deposit in the amount of $10,000. Suddenly, the company's debt-to-equity ratio rose from 2.26:1 to 3.36:1. The original debt structure was sound for this service business. Now owning its own real estate, the company looks weaker than when it was merely a tenant. On the surface, the debt structure appears to be too heavy for the size of the equity. But a look at any balance sheet is insufficient. The company had to prepare an earnings forecast before it bought the land and building. Favorable mortgage terms will permit the company to accomplish two objectives—increased profits and greater generation of cash or cash flow. However, because it is owning instead of renting its real estate, any future unsecured lender may become apprehensive about the company's ability to repay, considering the total present debt structure. Total liabilities immediately after purchase of the real estate in this illustration suddenly increased from $542,000 to $806,000. How misleading—when one considers that almost all of this new debt is deferred except for a tiny portion to be amortized quarterly.

Obviously the decision to buy was proper. The company made the mistake of buying directly instead of indirectly. A small company like this truck leasing company should purchase its real estate by having its stockholders acquire the real estate personally or in a separate corporate vehicle owned by the same stockholders.

ILLUSTRATION #1

TRUCK RENTER CORP.

BALANCE SHEET

BEFORE PURCHASE OF REAL ESTATE

ASSETS

Cash	$ 30,000
Accounts receivable	38,000
Inventory	4,000
Revenue-earning assets net of accumulated depreciation of $245,000	685,000
Prepaid expenses	15,000
Deposit as security	10,000
TOTAL ASSETS	**$782,000**

LIABILITIES AND STOCKHOLDERS' EQUITY

LIABILITIES

Accounts payable	$ 11,000
Notes payable secured by revenue-earning assets	489,000
Income taxes accrued	15,000
Expenses accrued	27,000
TOTAL LIABILITIES	**$542,000**

STOCKHOLDERS' EQUITY

Capital stock—1,000 shares $50 par value issued and outstanding	$ 50,000
Retained earnings	190,000
TOTAL STOCKHOLDERS' EQUITY	**$240,000**
TOTAL LIABILITIES AND STOCKHOLDERS' EQUITY	**$782,000**

See Accompanying Notes

NOTE: The company rents its premises under a lease from 19X2 to 19Y8 in the amount of $26,000 per annum to 19X9 and $30,000 per annum to 19Y8 plus increases in real estate taxes over base year 19X2, which amounted to $200 in 19X3.

ILLUSTRATION #2

TRUCK RENTER CORP.

BALANCE SHEET

AFTER PURCHASE OF REAL ESTATE

ASSETS

Cash	$ 10,000
Accounts receivable	38,000
Inventory	4,000
Revenue-earning assets net of accumulated depreciation of $245,000	685,000
Land	42,000
Building	252,000
Prepaid expenses	15,000
TOTAL ASSETS	**$1,046,000**

LIABILITIES AND STOCKHOLDERS' EQUITY

LIABILITIES

Accounts payable	$ 11,000
Notes payable secured by revenue-earning assets	489,000
First mortgage payable secured by land and building	264,000
Income taxes accrued	15,000
Expenses accrued	27,000
TOTAL LIABILITIES	**$ 806,000**

STOCKHOLDERS' EQUITY

Capital stock—1,000 shares $50 par value issued and outstanding	$ 50,000
Retained earnings	190,000
TOTAL STOCKHOLDERS' EQUITY	**$ 240,000**
TOTAL LIABILITIES AND STOCKHOLDERS' EQUITY	**$1,046,000**

See Accompanying Notes

NOTE: The real estate is recorded at cost. The building is to be depreciated over its useful life of thirty years. The first mortgage bears interest at the rate of seven and one-half percent per annum, with constant annual payments of interest and principal in the amount of $23,000 per annum.

BUY OR LEASE—WHAT YOU COULD HAVE RECOMMENDED TO THIS CLIENT

Set up a new company with adequate capital, here it is $30,000. A partnership is preferable (see Chapter 8 for a detailed explanation as to the tax ramifications of a partnership vs. a corporation). Be careful of a "thin" structure—too much debt to equity before your client takes the first step.

Your client would have had to obtain $30,000 from personal assets or other sources. Of course they could have borrowed the $30,000 from their truck leasing corporation, but they would have to ultimately repay the principal as well as pay a fair rate of interest on their debt to their own company.

The $30,000 would have been used by the new company as the down payment on the acquisition. The new company would then take title to the real estate. Now your client is his own landlord.

You should explain to your client that a separate real estate entity is preferable for the following reasons. First, the operations or truck-leasing aspect of the company is divorced from the real estate ownership aspect of the company. This divorce makes easier reading for the company's bankers, investment advisors or anyone needing to see the company's financials. There are no questions raised as to the ability of the company to pay off its mortgage. Obviously a successful company is easily able to pay its rent. Rarely will a prospective banker question the ability of a successful company to pay its rent. Furthermore, as long as the lease does not expire in the near term, there are no questions as to the cost of moving.

Second, the real estate has a value which is separate from the business. This value appears on the balance sheet only at the date of acquisition of the property. From that date forward the building is depreciated over its estimated useful life, but the building may actually increase in value. Demand for surrounding property may cause enhancement of realty values. Inflation of construction costs very likely may cause an increase in the value of the building. Yet, the balance sheet of the company reflects none of this. When the company owns its own real estate, an intelligent reader must separately analyze the value of the real estate. This analysis may be difficult if not impossible to make. For example, many publicly owned companies have purchased real estate in the last decade or two, only to find that values have doubled or tripled. Thus hidden assets are owned by these companies; they are hidden because the values on the balance sheet hide the real values.

Third, when a separate real estate entity is created, partners or stockholders have greater flexibility, assuming that the company is privately owned. At some future date they may desire to sell the property owned if it has appreciated in value. This becomes another opportunity to put capital gains dollars into their pockets at the best possible tax rates, depending upon the length of time the property is held. (See Chapter 8.)

HOW TO GET OUT PART OR ALL OF THE CASH INVESTED AND STILL OWN THE REAL ESTATE

Another maneuver well known to real estate professionals is known as "mortgaging out." This is an economic and tax ploy that works as follows:

The stockholders of your client, Truck Renter Corp., organize a new and separate partnership to acquire the real estate. Their corporation enters into an arm's-length lease with the partnership. The company pays rent to the partnership and the partnership amortizes the mortgage, paying interest and real estate taxes. After an appropriate period of time with increasing property values and a reduced mortgage, the partnership refinances the mortgage at a higher amount and puts the excess into the partners' pockets tax free. If this excess is equal to their original investment, the partners have "mortgaged out." If the excess is greater than their original investment, they have a cash "windfall" which is neither ordinary income nor capital gain. For income tax purposes this cash represents long-term borrowing, most of which may never be repaid. As long as the partners continue to own this real estate, there are no tax consequences in connection with this cash withdrawal. If at some later date the partners decide to sell this real estate, they will pay income taxes at the capital gains rates. Ownership of the realty will result in either ordinary income or loss, again depending on the circumstances. In the case of this truck rental company, let us assume that the stockholders have created a new partnership and examine the possibilities.

The partners personally invest $30,000 of cash into their partnership. The partnership buys the land and buildings at a total cost of $294,000, assuming a mortgage payable to the seller in the amount of $264,000. The terms of the mortgage call for constant annual payments in the amount of $23,000 with interest at 7½% per annum, payable quarterly.

The old rent is the same as before except that the partnership is the new landlord. From the viewpoint of this corporation nothing has changed. However the partners have gained the following advantages shown in Illustration # 3 on page 110.

In this first year of operating their own property they had a tax loss of $4,700. This loss is deductible for income tax purposes, depending on the tax bracket of the partners. An individual owner in the 50% bracket would save $2,350 in federal income taxes plus put $500 into his pocket. This combination of tax savings plus cash into pocket amounts to $2,850 cash generated in Year One from the $30,000 investment. Although most real estate investors look for higher yields, this yield of approximately 9.5% is satisfactory because the landlord and the tenant are the same person. Obviously at the expiration of the lease the tenant will be willing to pay a higher rent thus increasing the yield (assuming that the real estate has appreciated in value). If the real estate had not been purchased and the $30,000 had been invested by the partners in a savings account paying 10% per annum, their after-tax yield would have been only 5% or $1,500 for these owners in the 50% tax bracket.

The real yield on the property will arrive approximately six or seven years after acquisition.

In this illustration the investors should be able to recoup their original investment after the seventh year *plus* continue to take cash out of the real estate *plus* continue to take income tax losses as follows:

After seven years of amortization the mortgage is reduced to $235,882, a reduction of over $28,000. With normal mortgage

ILLUSTRATION #3

YEAR ONE

INCOME FOR TAX PURPOSES

Income		$ 26,200
Expenses		
Real estate taxes	$ 2,700	
Interest	19,800	
Depreciation	8,400	
TOTAL		30,900
Tax (loss)		$ (4,700)

INCOME FOR CASH PURPOSES

Income		$ 26,200
Expenses		
Real estate taxes	$ 2,700	
Interest and amortization of		
First Mortgage	23,000	
Total cash expenses		25,700
CASH INCOME		$ 500

markets and the usual supply of money available, the investors should be able to negotiate a more favorable mortgage, probably back to $264,000. Thus they could put $30,000 back into their pockets tax-free.

One problem: their after-tax percent yield would decline during this seven-year period due to the decrease in the income tax loss.

Year	Percent Yield	Amortization
1	9.5	$3,200
2	9.1	3,440
3	8.7	3,698
4	8.2	3,975
5	7.7	4,273
6	7.2	4,594
7	6.7	4,938

This seems to be a small price to pay to get all of the investment out after the seventh year. Only a real estate professional might seek to get his money out earlier.

When a service business owns its own real estate and the business is incorporated, there are still certain tactics which your client can employ. One approach is to spin off the real estate and related mortgages payable into a separate real estate subsidiary. This provides users with a better analysis. The tax consequences of every step must be measured, however. For example, New York City presently imposes a tax on rent even if it is paid to a wholly owned subsidiary. Many corporations operating in New York City merged their real estate subsidiaries into their operating subsidiaries, thereby eliminating the rent and related tax.

Another tactic used by an incorporated service business to recover an original investment in its own real estate is proper refinancing. If real estate has increased in value substantially since acquisition, in many instances the mortgage can be refinanced or a second mortgage placed on the property. In these circumstances the corporation must be sure that it can amortize a greater debt load, pay higher interest rates or both.

WHICH SERVICE BUSINESSES SHOULD OWN THEIR
REAL ESTATE AND WHY

Certain service businesses should own their own real estate if adequate capital is invested in the operations or financing is available.

My guide to the buy or rent decision is: If real estate is an essential part of the service provided, the business is in a better economic posture when it owns rather than rents. This is true for two reasons. First, the business should not be subject to the risks incidental to renting. For example, if the business had to move at the expiration of a lease, the business might risk impairment or destruction. Second, the business should be able to exercise control over the real estate. Certain structures are specifically designed to house certain types of service businesses. An independent real estate investor is reluctant to invest in such specialty type real estate. When the real estate investor does decide to invest in such real estate, the investor must obtain a higher than normal rate of return on his investment.

The service businessman whose service is related to real estate should not be penalized by being forced to pay an unreasonably high rent to an independent investor. It is more profitable to own and to finance if your client has the funds available or access to the funds needed for a down payment.

The following service businesses should own rather then rent:

- Bowling Alleys
- Car Washes
- Funeral Directors
- Hospitals (Proprietary)
- Hotels and Motels
- Laundries and Dry Cleaners (Factory)
- Nursing Homes (Proprietary)
- Real Estate Investment
- Storage and Warehousing
- Television and Radio Broadcasting

Bowling Alleys

Successful bowling alleys operate in buildings specifically designed for bowling. The equity of the owner is in the equipment. The service performed (rent) primarily consists in renting an alley to the public. Secondary services include rental of shoes, balls, and so on. Sales of food and beverages are also secondary in that the customers are in the bowling alley primarily to bowl. The bowling business is a cash business and is difficult to manage unless ownership and management are one and the same.

From the viewpoint of a real estate investor, a bowling alley tenant is not a strong tenant. He doesn't have a strong balance sheet. Therefore real estate investors normally are reluctant to rent to a bowling alley operator if the property is free-standing and is to be tailor-made for bowling. A good operator accordingly should seek to purchase or build his own property. If he has his building built for him he may be able to obtain mortgage financing from the builder. He should attempt to split his equity between the equipment and the real estate. Some shopping center owners build bowling alleys as part of the complex of buildings. In those cases the operator is a tenant. It is recommended that such tenants obtain long-term leases to protect themselves from the owner. A good manager, once he has developed a successful bowling alley operation, would not be able to move outside of the shopping center complex. He is therefore in a weak bargaining position if he has a short-term lease.

If the bowling alley operator plans to buy the real estate, it is important that a separate entity be created or that individuals own the real estate in their own names.

Car Washes

Car washes are either free-standing or integrated with a related business such as a garage, gasoline station, and so on. Car washes require an investment in equipment especially designed to speed the car through the washing and drying process. This type of business is most profitable in an area that is easily accessible to automobiles. Usually the car moves through the washing system. Many small one-story buildings can be converted into car-washing operations.

The real estate is essential to the car washing business. Therefore the operator of the car wash business should own the real estate. Ownership should be segregated from the operation in a separate entity or be individually owned.

Hotels and Motels

The decision to own or to rent the real estate in this field is based on three factors:

Capital—if adequate capital is available, the decision is usually to own. Proper mortgage financing is important. The smaller hotel or motel owner can rarely obtain an investor to rent the real estate to him.

Operating ability—if an operating company is successful, it can usually induce an investor to own and lease the real estate to it. Successful operators also can sell owned real estate and take back a lease.

A franchise—many well-known hotel and motel chains sell franchises. The franchisee is nearly always required to own the real estate.

Real estate maneuvering is attractive in the hotel and motel field. For example, the land could be owned by one company, the building by a second company and the business of innkeeping done by a third company.

The difference between success and failure in hotel and motel operation is the decision whether to own or to rent, because the service rendered is directly related to the real estate, its cost, financing, location, maintenance and refurbishing. A hotel or motel operator who owns the land and building gains considerable flexibility over his counterpart who is simply a tenant.

Laundries and Dry Cleaners

The success of a laundry or dry cleaning service business is normally not related to the ownership or rental of its real estate.

Dry cleaning businesses are divided into five categories—a factory, a store serviced by a factory, a chain (a factory that runs its own stores), a store that does its own dry cleaning, and a store with coin-operated dry cleaning equipment. Real estate plays an important role in the operations of a factory. Ownership here is integral to successful operations. The other four categories of the dry cleaning business should not invest capital in real estate. Of course every rule has its exception. The drive-in type of dry cleaning store that is free-standing should own its real estate because the real estate is vital to its success.

The dry cleaner must invest in his specialized type of equipment. His success is related to the quality of his work with this equipment. Usually space can be rented for a long term in a small store already constructed by a real estate investor. A successful operator whose capital is not tied up in real estate can rent other stores and conduct business in more than one location. Therefore it is preferable to rent rather than own.

Nursing Homes

Nursing homes and extended care facilities are service businesses that should own real estate. Nursing homes today must meet standards and specifications prescribed by various local governments. Therefore new buildings are "tailor-made" to satisfy these requirements and provide a satisfactory return on investment. In prior years it was economically feasible to convert a building into a nursing home. Now that procedure is not economically feasible in most cases.

Operators of nursing homes should own the real estate separately. The nursing home operation is usually incorporated for legal purposes. It rents the land and building or only the land from another entity formed by the nursing home operator.

Since the Federal government reimburses nursing homes

through Medicare and Medicaid plus local governmental or private plan reimbursements, nursing home accounting is rigidly prescribed, as we shall see in Chapter 5.

Real Estate Investment

If your client is a real estate operator, you should advise him that he must own not rent real estate. The service he provides is occupancy by another of his real estate. In the event that the investor is unable to acquire title to the real property in its entirety, he has five other options open to him as follows:

1. Ownership of land only
2. Ownership of building only
3. Leasehold right to land and building
4. Leasehold right to land
5. Leasehold right to building

Again we have the exceptions to the rule. Leasehold rights are not the rights of ownership. Usually real estate investors who acquire leasehold rights acquire the equivalent of ownership with a long-term lease. The owner usually transfers the rights of ownership during the leased period. A ninety-nine year lease, for example, effectively transfers ownership rights depending on the terms of the lease.

Real estate properties are usually either commercial or residential. However, some buildings are designed as combination residential and commercial. There are three basic combinations. First, inner-city office buildings today are sometimes designed for residential tenants in tower floors. Second, some homeowners have converted their residences partially into commercial space. Finally, there is the "taxpayer." This term describes a two-story building with stores or offices on the ground floor and apartments on the second floor.

Real estate financials are fully described in Chapters 1, 2 and 3. Special accounting forms are more fully explained in Chapter 6.

Storage and Warehousing

This service business has many aspects that are similar to real estate investment, especially to operators of office buildings. Most storage and warehousing companies are also engaged in the moving business, which is another type of service.

Ownership of the warehouse is essential to this business. Storage rentals and warehouse rentals are typically so low per square foot of space that the operator in this service business must own. He cannot afford to rent the building from an investor because he must charge a low rental.

Many companies in the moving business accumulate capital and form their own storage and warehousing businesses. The process is a natural one because the warehousing and storage function requires the moving or trucking of whatever has to be stored.

If a moving or trucking company forms a storage and warehouse business, a separate entity should be formed to own the real estate. The individuals owning the moving or trucking company need to control and measure the profitability of the warehouse business. Either a separate division or corporation should be organized to segregate costs, expenses and income related to the warehouse. However, the individuals should own the real estate directly or in a separate real estate corporation.

As real estate owners, the warehouse owners will probably have a low return on their investment. But the separate warehouse operating division of a moving business should be profitable. To measure their real return on investment, the owners should add back their warehousing profits to the earnings solely arising from the real estate. In other words, the owners of the warehouse cannot consider that they have a passive realty investment. They are in the warehouse operating business. The investment in the warehouse land and building was made to set up an operating business. Therefore, the rate of return on investment includes the return from the warehouse operating business as well as the return from the piece of real estate which is the warehouse.

Funeral Directors

Funeral directors are licensed professionals, but real estate is essential to their business. The functions of the funeral home (mortuary) are threefold:

First, it is the place where the deceased reposes and is prepared for burial.

Second, space is provided for the family of the deceased to receive visitors.

Third, space is provided (a chapel or other suitable area) for the funeral service.

There is no room for a professional real estate investor's profit. Furthermore, the building is altered or specially erected for this business. Therefore, the business must own the land and building. The stockholders, partners or proprietor should acquire the real estate personally, which they should rent to their operating company. Again, personal ownership provides more flexibility for future sale, expansion or financing.

Traditionally this service business is a family business. In many instances a large residence is acquired and converted into a mortuary. Sometimes a building is specially constructed. Adequate land is required for parking. Mortgage financing is usually available.

Due to the professional aspects of this business, there is less room to maneuver this type of real estate.

Television and Radio Broadcasting

Real estate is essential to television and radio broadcasting, but in a limited aspect. The antenna equipment should be erected on real estate owned by the operator. The antenna is built to specification in accordance with the requirements of the Federal Communications Commission (FCC). The location is important and should be controlled by the broadcaster. If the antenna is isolated geographically, the land should be owned. In major metropolitan areas such as New York City, antennas have been located atop skyscrapers that are usually owned by others.

All of the broadcasting facilities, including the transmitter, studio, administration and sales department, may be housed in rented quarters. Some stations rent space in office buildings. Where a radio or television station operator owns and occupies the major part of an office building, space can be rented to others.

Most of the stations acquire the real estate they occupy. It is preferable to segregate all of the land and buildings in a separate real estate entity. In many operations, this is not feasible.

The decision to own or rent is complex due to the following factors:

1. **License.** If the license is granted by the FCC to an individual or group for a new station, all the facilities must be created. This situation affords the most flexibility. A separate real estate entity can be created to own the land and building or buildings.

   If the license is transferred from one operator to another, it may not be possible or preferable to create a separate real estate entity. Usually income tax considerations will prevail. The purchaser will want to assign as much of the purchase price as possible to depreciable assets. If the purchase price exceeds book value, as it usually does, the real estate becomes important. The book value of the real estate is normally undervalued. Consequently the purchaser looks first to the real estate in order to assign a fair market value out of the total purchase price. Even if the seller of the station owned the real estate individually or in a separate vehicle, the purchaser will try to telescope down the amount of goodwill that must be recorded on the purchaser's books. Presently, goodwill must be written off over forty years when acquired, but there is no income tax expense for goodwill allowable as a deduction against taxable income. Therefore, the purchaser will try to maximize the real estate value that he records on acquisition to obtain the highest possible depreciation charges.

2. **Ownership of the purchaser** is another factor influencing the buy or rent decision. If the purchaser is publicly owned

or plans to "go public," the purchaser obtains no benefit in creating a separate real estate owning entity. This is due to the difference in economic and tax goals of a public vs. a privately held company. A private owner usually seeks to minimize federal income taxes while removing as much of the cash profits as possible for the benefit of the stockholders. This is rarely a major goal of a publicly held company.

Hospitals

The operators of proprietary hospitals should own the land and building. The building is essential to the professional services provided. All proprietary as well as voluntary hospitals are regulated by various governmental agencies. All hospitals must conform to standards and specifications prescribed by these agencies. New hospitals are "tailor-made" to satisfy those requirements and provide a satisfactory return on investment.

Most proprietary hospitals are created by a doctor or group of doctors. The business has become so profitable that publicly owned companies are entering the field.

Usually a group of doctors with different specialties acquire a piece of real estate and simultaneously create a hospital. The hospital is incorporated for legal purposes. The doctors should own the real estate separately while leasing it back at an arm's length basis to the corporation. In some states, like New York, separate ownership may be almost impossible.

Separate ownership of the real estate affords considerable flexibility to the originating group of doctors. Young competent doctors with little capital can join other doctors with large amounts of capital. Doctors who have larger amounts of capital can obtain a greater equity in the real estate than they may have in the operations of the hospital.

Many different types of financing are available for hospital real estate because hospitals are in demand and in the public interest. Local governments usually encourage construction of hospital facilities.

Outside of New York in the last decade, a trend has begun towards the publicly owned hospital corporation.

In prior years it has been possible to convert very large residences into a hospital. With increasing regulation this type of approach is not economically feasible.

Hospital accounting is rigidly prescribed, as has been outlined in Chapters 1, 2, and 3, because of the many governmental and private plan (Blue Cross type) reimbursement requirements.

HOW YOUR CLIENT CAN OWN REAL ESTATE AND DIVORCE HIMSELF FROM PERSONAL MORTGAGE LIABILITY

The service businessman planning to buy a piece of real estate should consult his attorney. However, there is a simple rule that your client should follow from the business and tax viewpoint:

Do not guarantee personally any mortgage on the real estate.

Financial institutions rely primarily on the value of the real estate to secure the funds they lend in connection with the mortgage bond or note. Usually the lending institution will insist that the mortgage instrument of indebtedness be signed and guaranteed.

Personal guarantees by the service businessman himself can be avoided in several ways, depending on how the lending institution wants to complete the financing transaction. At this point it is important to bear in mind that there are complex tax, economic and legal consequences.

DUMMY OR CONDUIT CORPORATION

Many real estate deals are completed by incorporating a special purpose corporation with no assets or liabilities. No stock is issued and no cash is contributed to capital. The corporation is inactive in all respects, earning no income and incurring no expenses. The corporation is alive for only one moment and is then dissolved. The sole function of the "conduit" corporation is to take title to the real estate without any consideration and sign the mortgage bond. It immediately transfers title to the individual purchaser or partnership.

THE STRAW MAN

The "straw man" is a real man or woman who for a fee performs the same functions as the "conduit" corporation. That is, he or she signs the mortgage note or bond. There are people who are willing to perform this task and that is their primary business. Only the name of the "straw man" appears on the mortgage bond. He takes title to the property solely for the purpose of signing the mortgage bond and immediately transfers title to the real owner or owners.

THE EXCULPATORY CLAUSE

Some financial institutions are willing to waive all personal liability and will allow the mortgage bond to omit liability in a special clause in the mortgage instrument. This clause is known as the "exculpatory" clause. The real owner may take title directly and the institution will look only to the real estate for security.

REAL ESTATE—AN APPRAISAL OF THE VARIOUS TYPES OF DEBT INSTRUMENTS A SERVICE BUSINESS SHOULD USE

Purchase Money Mortgage—This type of borrowing is usually very reasonable, especially when money markets are tight and financing is difficult. Typically, the businessman who wants to purchase real estate when he acquires a service business can obtain favorable financing from the seller. The seller, usually to induce the purchaser to buy his service business, will take back what is known as a purchase money mortgage as part of the consideration for the sale of the real estate. In many deals this type of mortgage, which is in lieu of part of the cash purchase price, comes after and is subordinate to an existing first mortgage held by a financial institution. Most purchase money mortgages require a shorter period of amortization than an existing first mortgage. The customary period is three to ten years. Each deal is structured differently, depending upon the economic and tax posture of the seller.

First Mortgage—This type of financing has a first lien on the property. It is commonly used in the following situations:

The Service Business is erecting its own building on owned land. It should secure a first mortgage from a financial institution.

The Service Business is purchasing an existing business with real estate. If the first mortgage can be refinanced favorably, especially if the company can increase the amount of the mortgage to meet its needs, it should do so.

Financing is a major problem for many smaller service businesses that should own their own real estate. Some businesses solve this problem by entering into a long-term lease. Usually the rent is high in this type of situation. In effect, the service businessman is parting with some of his profits that he could have retained if he had adequate capital to acquire the real estate needed to operate his business.

Second Mortgage—Many times your client will be able to acquire a good piece of property by borrowing and allowing the lender to place a secondary lien on the real estate. Sometimes a third or fourth mortgage is placed. However, you should advise your client that too much debt greatly increases the risk. If business conditions worsen, your client may not be able to pay the interest or amortization where the debt load is too great. Your client could lose his investment if the holder of the mortgage has to foreclose.

THE BUILDER AS A SOURCE OF FUNDS

In some cases a builder may be a source of funds. The typical arrangement is as follows: The builder buys land or has land in his inventory. The builder arranges the construction financing related to his own financial resources invested in the property. The builder sells the completed building and land to the service business at a substantial profit. The builder takes back a purchase money mortgage as part of the sales price of the real estate.

This arrangement has many variations. For example, if the service businessman does not have adequate capital funds available for a down payment to buy when construction is completed, the builder may rent and grant a short-term option to buy. These options typically run for a period of years with a fixed purchase price agreed upon before the term of the lease begins.

FINANCING FROM GOVERNMENT

Government financing is available in many circumstances. The Small Business Administration and state and local governments have various types of financing plans at very attractive rates of interest and unusually favorable amortization. The problem with government financing is that invariably it takes an unreasonably long time to process the loan application. Nevertheless, this type of financing is usually most beneficial. Your client should always consult legal counsel. Almost all of these governmental agencies require that the borrower prepare a forecast of earnings and cash flow over an extended time, setting forth exactly how the borrower intends to repay the loan.

OVERINSURANCE

Many service businessmen are reluctant to take title to real property in their personal names because of potential liability. There is a simple solution to this problem—overinsurance.

Overinsurance or excess insurance is a small price to pay for protection against liability. Of course there are exceptions to this rule and an attorney should be consulted. For example, in a hospital where life and death are involved in the day-to-day operation of the service business, the real estate should be owned in a separate corporate entity. Liability is, accordingly, limited.

Insurance costs are significant, but insurance is mandatory. Clients who own real estate personally or in partnership should have more coverage than they would normally have if they owned their real estate indirectly through a corporate vehicle. This incremental cost of insurance is usually a minor factor in the overall expense structure of the operations.

TO SUM UP

When a service company owns its own real estate, it looks weaker because its debt-to-equity ratio is greater. The solution to this is to have your client own his own real estate separately. Furthermore, the real estate has a separate economic value. If the value increases, it can be sold or refinanced and the business will still continue.

If real estate is an essential part of the service provided, the business is in a better economic picture when it owns rather than rents. Be sure that if your client decides to buy that he does not guarantee personally any mortgage on the real estate.

Help him with the right financing and check out his insurance coverage carefully, especially when he is not sheltered by the corporate cloak.

5

Using Income Statement Analysis as a Measure of Performance

HOW TO PREPARE A TREND ANALYSIS

One of the most helpful tools you can create for your client is an Analysis of Income Statement Trends.

Simply place the income statement of one period next to another over a significant time frame in order to be able to compare income and expenses. Be sure that expenses are classified on a comparable basis.

Usually certain expenses change from one time frame to another. For example, payroll categories may change. It is important to reclassify expenses retroactively where feasible and meaningful. If you are unable to do this, then you should group the expenses into a more generic classification. If "stationery" is becoming a more significant expense, but if you are unable to ascertain prior period amounts, you may have to group "stationery" with other "office supplies."

Most of your clients should have either monthly or quarterly financial statements. The monthly income statement is preferable because of timing and accuracy. If you watch a monthly trend you will spot a problem sooner than if you watch a quarterly trend. Also, an account that you may want to examine and analyze in depth may be buried by the other two monthly numbers if you watch a quarterly trend. You may fail therefore to spot a problem at all. If your client has been in business for a number of years, you can set up yearly and quarterly trends as well as monthly trends. If your client has been in business only a short time, then a yearly trend analysis may not be feasible or significant.

Trend analysis will help your client spot expenses which are increasing disproportionately. You can do this in two ways—in dollars or in percentages. If the expense rises sharply in either dollars or as a percent of sales, watch out. Keep in mind that the increase may be due to a seasonal variance. Illustrations #1 and #2 show how useful the monthly trend analysis can be in spotting potential problems.

HOW TO SAVE TIME EVALUATING TRENDS

In Illustration #1 we have a short series of income statements, almost too short to see a trend. However in the first month, January, promotion expense was in the amount of $3,700. By June, promotion expense had climbed 140% to $8,900. This type of change is easily spotted if the trend analysis is over a long enough period. The key to evaluation is to spot the major variance or change, either up or down.

As shown in Illustration #2, operating overhead in January was 23.5% and fell to 23.0% in June due to an increase in fees earned in the amount of $15,900 (125,600—$109,700). The variance of 0.5% is an indicator. But it isn't really saying that any drastic change has occurred.

Payroll and related fringe costs as a percent of income

ILLUSTRATION #1
JUST AND ABLE, ATTORNEYS
INCOME STATEMENT
MONTHLY TREND

	January	February	March	April	May	June
Fees Earned	$109,700	$111,800	$117,000	$124,000	$121,900	$125,600
Payroll:						
Direct	26,100	26,700	27,600	29,000	29,000	29,100
Indirect	4,900	4,900	5,200	5,100	5,000	5,200
Payroll Fringe Costs	3,600	3,600	3,700	3,900	3,900	3,900
	34,600	35,200	36,500	38,000	37,900	38,200
Net Fees	75,100	76,600	80,500	86,000	84,000	87,400
Operating Overhead:						
Computer service	1,200	1,000	1,200	1,500	1,400	1,500
Depreciation	3,400	3,400	3,400	3,400	3,400	3,400
Insurance	2,800	2,800	2,800	2,900	2,900	2,900
Miscellaneous	200	100	400	300	100	300
Office supplies	3,400	3,000	2,900	3,600	2,500	2,300
Periodicals and books	700	200	500	900	700	600
Postage	300	300	200	300	300	300
Professional service	800	900	700	1,800	800	900
Promotion	3,700	4,800	4,000	6,000	7,900	8,900
Rent	4,700	4,700	4,700	4,700	4,700	4,700
Reproducing expenses	400	300	400	500	400	400
Telephone and telegraph	900	800	700	800	700	800
Training costs	1,800	1,100	500	1,600	1,000	600
Travel	1,100	1,000	900	1,100	1,000	900
Utilities	400	400	500	400	400	400
Total Operating Expenses	25,800	24,800	23,800	29,800	28,200	28,900
NET INCOME	$ 49,300	$ 51,800	$ 56,700	$ 56,200	$ 55,800	$ 58,500

ILLUSTRATION #2

JUST AND ABLE, ATTORNEYS

INCOME STATEMENT

EXPRESSED IN PERCENTAGES

MONTHLY TREND

	Jan.	Feb.	Mar.	Apr.	May	Jun.
Fees Earned	100.0	100.0	100.0	100.0	100.0	100.0
Payroll:						
Direct	23.8	23.9	23.6	23.4	23.8	23.2
Indirect	4.5	4.4	4.4	4.1	4.1	4.1
Payroll Fringe						
Costs	3.3	3.2	3.2	3.1	3.2	3.1
Total	31.6	31.5	31.2	30.6	31.1	30.4
Net Fees	68.4	68.5	68.8	69.4	68.9	69.6
Operating						
Overhead	23.5	22.2	20.3	24.0	23.1	23.0
NET INCOME	44.9	46.3	48.5	45.4	45.8	46.6

actually fell from 31.6% to 30.4%. This change partially explains the increase in firm net income.

Further analysis should be done of the "promotion" account in order to control the expense. Are there any surprises or anticipated items? Were expenses properly approved? How much was budgeted for the year for promotion? How does the budget for promotion compare to the actual expense incurred? All of these questions should be answered in an examination of the accounts.

Notice that the financials are presented on the accrual basis for this legal firm in Illustration #1. Fees earned each month should include fee discounts or write-downs. Some law firms prefer to set up "fees earned" at standard rates. Then write-downs, discounts or variances would be set forth separately on another line.

DISBURSEMENT CONTROL AND ANALYSIS

Most law firms segregate charges from reimbursement of out-of-pocket expenses. Other firms credit this income directly to the expense account. The best control is to have the payment by the law firm charged to an asset account usually called "disbursements." When the client is billed, the disbursements account is credited and a new asset account is created called "disbursements receivable." Most clients pay attorneys for out-of-pocket (OOP) expenses. Therefore it is unrealistic to show the recovery of these expenses as "income."

The firm also can see how much it has failed to charge to its clients when the item is debited to the asset. If disbursements cannot be identified, they have to be expensed. Uncollectible receivables will also have to be written off. In Illustration #1, the postage expense is averaging about $300 per month. This OOP expense should be close to zero each month. Is the law firm missing billings to certain clients? Obviously a law firm this large has some non-chargeable postage. Is the $300 a budgeted number? If so, what constitutes "administration postage"?

OPERATIONAL DECISIONS

When the financial statements are prepared and set up to show trends, all of the out-of-pocket expenses can be monitored for deviances. One important result could be the reclassification of certain non-chargeable expenses to chargeable. Here you can help your client make more money. For example, your law firm client may see that too many OOP expenses are being borne by the firm. Since most clients do not balk at paying "disbursements" of the law firms, some of these "disbursements" may be adjusted to recover OOP costs. Most law firms have a standard charge for copying such as ten cents per sheet or twenty cents per sheet. Their rental OOP costs may be five cents per sheet but they are recovering part or all of the labor cost involved in making copies.

Let's look at another illustration which could lead to an

operational decision by the law firm of Just and Able. Here in Illustration #3 is a trend of a single expense, "computer service," from January to the end of September. The trend is up at a rate which is not satisfactory. If the trend line continues in the same direction after September, then action is needed unless the client's budget called for such an increase in accordance with the planned needs of the firm. In fact, the trend line signalled a problem at the end of July.

ILLUSTRATION #3

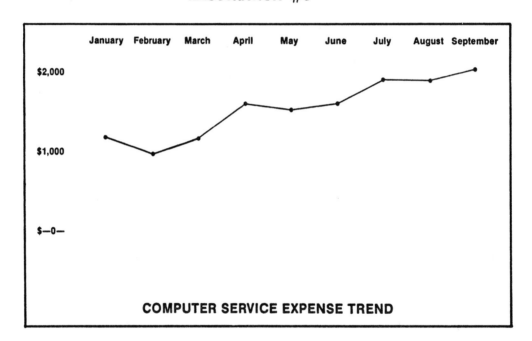

COMPUTER SERVICE EXPENSE TREND

This situation points up why a company budget is so important. What did your client expect to spend on computer service for the year? And how much was allocated to each month or quarter? Under certain conditions, the trend could be considered satisfactory; for example, if the law firm has a practice which is seasonal and computer service needs are increased later in the year. Chapter 9 shows how budgets are used to maintain costs.

Let's assume that your client was willing to spend $7,200 on computer services during the first six months of the year. The actual expense was $7,800. Your client asks, "What can we do to cut this cost?"

You have to ascertain what caused this expense to exceed the budget. Once you have determined the cause, you can provide the answer to the client's question. There are many alternative courses of action to cost cutting at this point.

1. Reevaluate your client's needs and review the problem with the company.
2. Reduce the input into the computer.
3. Reduce the output from the computer.
4. Change computer service companies.
5. Lease computer equipment.
6. Purchase computer equipment.
7. Shift from computer to manual.
8. Review the problem with a consultant.
9. Bring in another public accounting firm to review the problem.
10. Talk to the appropriate committee of your State CPA Society or AICPA.

Let's look at Illustration #1 again. The largest single item of expense in this or any law firm is payroll. In four months, the payroll increased approximately 11% from $26,100 to $29,100, or $3,000. The payroll continued at this level in May and June. You should ask, "Why?" If overtime is constant and is the primary cause of the increase, then an analysis is in order. First, see what payroll has been budgeted. Should the firm hire additional associates or clerical employees to eliminate any need for substantial overtime? If the payroll increase was due to retention of new employees you should review where they fit into the chart of organization. It is evident that the fees earned increased on a quarter-to-quarter basis. Fees averaged about $11,000 per month more during the quarter ended June 30 than the quarter ended March 31. Fees averaged $124,000 per month in the second quarter. Obviously the increase in workload had to be accompanied by a higher payroll.

USING FLASH INCOME STATEMENTS TO
SIMPLIFY INTERIM CONTROL

In service businesses there are shortcuts you can take to prepare simple income statements due to the nature of most service businesses. Because the operating overhead tends to be fairly stable in service businesses, it is a relatively easy matter to prepare a simple income statement. Let's go back to the law firm in Illustration #1. Most payroll is fixed on an annual basis with the exceptions of overtime or hourly work, bonuses, vacation pay, holiday pay or sick pay. If payroll and related fringe costs in the year prior to Illustration #1 averaged $35,000 per month and operating overhead averaged $26,000 per month, a simple income statement could be prepared each month as soon as fees earned had been determined. Using these facts, Illustration #4 shows what the simple income statement would reveal prior to preparation of an actual monthly or quarterly set of financials.

ILLUSTRATION #4

JUST AND ABLE, ATTORNEYS

FLASH INCOME STATEMENT

ESTIMATED

	Jan.	Feb.	Mar.	Apr.	May	Jun.
Fees Earned	$109,700	$111,800	$117,000	$124,000	$121,900	$125,600
Payroll and related fringes	35,000	35,000	35,000	35,000	35,000	35,000
NET FEES	74,700	76,800	82,000	89,000	86,900	90,600
Operating overhead	26,000	26,000	26,000	26,000	26,000	26,000
NET INCOME	$ 48,700	$ 50,800	$ 56,000	$ 63,000	$ 60,900	$ 64,600

A refinement of the flash income statement appears in Illustration #5. Here we still show average operating overhead of $26,000 per month. However, in most law firms, a separate record is kept of payroll, and usually a separate bank account is maintained for payroll. Therefore it should be a fairly simple matter to obtain the actual payroll expense and related fringe costs immediately after the month ends. This has been done in Illustration #5.

ILLUSTRATION #5

JUST AND ABLE, ATTORNEYS

FLASH INCOME STATEMENT

ESTIMATED

	Jan.	Feb.	Mar.	Apr.	May	Jun.
Fees Earned	$109,700	$111,800	$117,000	$124,000	$121,900	$125,600
Payroll and related fringes	34,600	35,200	36,500	38,000	37,900	38,200
NET FEES	75,100	76,600	80,500	86,000	84,000	87,400
Operating overhead	26,000	26,000	26,000	26,000	26,000	26,000
NET INCOME	$ 49,100	$ 50,600	$ 54,500	$ 60,000	$ 58,000	$ 61,400

Essentially, the simple income statement or flash income statement is only an approximation of net income. When the actual information is available, a proper set of financials may be produced. Compare Illustration #1 with Illustration #5. You can see the variances due to estimating. Many small businesses only prepare actual financials quarterly. For these businesses, it would be more informative to prepare a flash income statement similar to Illustration #5 for the first and second months of the quarterly period.

Some businesses like to have weekly flash reports. The pro-

ILLUSTRATION #6

JUST AND ABLE, ATTORNEYS

QUARTERLY INCOME STATEMENTS

	First Quarter	Second Quarter	Increase or (Decrease)	Percentage Change
Fees Earned	$338,500	$371,500	$ 33,000	
Payroll:				
Direct	80,400	87,100	6,700	8.33%
Indirect	15,000	15,300	300	2.0
Payroll Fringe Costs	10,900	11,700	800	7.34
Total	106,300	114,100	7,800	
Net Fees	232,200	257,400	25,200	
Operating Overhead:				
Computer Services	3,400	4,400	1,000	29.41
Depreciation	10,200	10,200	—	—
Insurance	8,400	8,700	300	3.57
Miscellaneous	700	700	—	—
Office Supplies	9,300	8,400	(900)	—
Postage	800	900	100	12.50
Periodicals and Books	1,400	2,200	800	57.14
Professional Services	2,400	3,500	1,100	45.83
Promotion	12,500	22,800	10,300	82.40
Rent	14,100	14,100	—	—
Reproducing Expenses	1,100	1,300	200	18.18
Telephone and Telegraph ..	2,400	2,300	(100)	—
Training Costs	3,400	3,200	(200)	—
Travel	3,000	3,000	—	—
Utilities	1,300	1,200	(100)	—
Total Operating Expenses	74,400	86,900	12,500	
NET INCOME	$157,800	$170,500	$ 12,700	

cedure to prepare reports weekly is similar to preparing Illustration #5 monthly. Earnings and payroll are accumulated weekly and operating overhead is estimated on a weekly basis. Of course you can do the same estimating if your client wants daily flash reports. Then at the end of each week you can total the dailies into a weekly flash report.

TROUBLESHOOTING PROBLEMS THROUGH MANAGEMENT-BY-EXCEPTION REPORTING ON INCOME STATEMENTS

Let us see how to monitor the significant costs of doing business using the management-by-exception approach to the income statement. The idea is to save time when pinpointing problems.

Here is the concept: Only spend your time reviewing the exceptions. For example, compare the actual with the budget income statement. Analyze only the exceptions. If there is no budget and you are having difficulty in convincing your client to set one up, then compare the actual to actual, from one period to another, and analyze only the exceptions. Let's see how Illustration #7 shows the exceptions when it is condensed into a quarterly format as we have set forth in Illustration #6. It is apparent from a quick scanning of the column headed "Increase" (or "Decrease") that there are a few exceptions to the norm. Five expense categories have increased out of proportion where the dollars involved are significant to total expenses.

The following five exceptions listed in Illustration #7 should be analyzed.

**ILLUSTRATION #7
EXCEPTIONS**

		Percent Increase
Payroll—Direct	$ 6,700	8.33%
Computer Services	1,000	29.41
Periodicals and Books	800	57.14
Professional Services	1,100	45.83
Promotion	10,300	82.40
	$19,900	

These five are significant because of the percentage changes from quarter to quarter as well as the fact that their dollar expense is material in relation to the total operating expenses and payroll of the law firm. In fact, the two largest items, Payroll —Direct $6,700 and Promotion $10,300, total $17,000, which represents a major part of the total expense increase. Analysis therefore should begin with these two items. Why did they increase so dramatically?

Using the management-by-exception approach, you point at these five expenses out of the eighteen expenses and costs for follow-up action. You can refine it even further with the two major items, Payroll—Direct and Promotion. You should indicate to your client to look first at the exceptions each quarter or each month—as often as financials are prepared for management.

The income statement can also be viewed from the top rather than the bottom. Depending upon your client's business, you can take the management-by-exception approach to the "income" aspect rather than the "expense" aspect of the income statement. For example, if your client owns and operates vending equipment such as a laundromat or any coin-operated unit, you should have him record income from each unit separately, that is, each piece of equipment as well as the group. Total income could then be averaged. In the event that income per unit for a given location declines sharply from one period to another, action must be taken. It may be that someone is stealing from the location where there is such a fall-off in income. Here again, management looks at the exception. Locations that are producing normally do not require management action. This is really a market analysis type of problem. It is essential that your client understand his market.

HOW TO REVISE AN INCOME STATEMENT FOR BETTER MANAGEMENT CONTROL

Too many financials of service businesses are not useful tools primarily because they are on the cash basis rather than on the accrual basis.

Service businesses generally employ the accrual basis for

financial statement presentation. Personal service companies or individuals such as accountants, lawyers, dentists, doctors, architects, public relations people, management consultants and others tend to use cash-basis financials for both management and tax reporting purposes. Accordingly, they are unable to measure adequately income and related expenses. Chapter 8 covers a simple solution to the conversion from cash basis to accrual basis.

The most difficult area of conversion from cash-basis record keeping to accrual basis is the problem of "income." Many professionals feel that only when they have been paid can they truly report their fees as income. Possibly for some beginners this may be so, but it is not valid for most professionals. Routinely, two types of "income" problems affect professionals— the "if" and the "when."

The "when" problem is easier. When the service is rendered to the client or patient, income is earned. Time charges should be recorded as work-in-process until an invoice is submitted. If there is an agreement or understanding before the service is rendered as to the terms of payment, the "when" is reduced simply to the recording of in-process time charges, the ultimate billing and collection process. Some professionals require an advance fee or retainer before the services are actually rendered or during the period the services are being performed. Billing and collection procedures vary, depending upon the nature and length of the services to be performed as well as the ability of the client to pay and the amount of the fee. Of course there will be exceptions to almost every rule such as the contingency fee arrangement by a law firm that primarily has retainer clients.

The "if" problem is not so easy to resolve. It boils down to discounts (write-downs from billed amounts or from standard fee rates) or write-offs of fees deemed uncollectible. The best way to resolve the "if" problem is to obtain a retainer in advance of the service to be performed. In the event that this approach cannot be used, then the invoice that is rendered should be in an amount which may be reasonably anticipated to be collected. If there is a problem due to the accumulation of too much work-in-process time which cannot be billed, then the excess should be written off before the actual invoice is rendered.

Most personal service businesses keep track of time either

manually or through a computer. Timekeeping is usually done at pre-arranged standard rates.

Over a significant time frame, it is possible to estimate an overall discount rate from standard fees charged. If work-in-process is recorded at standard rates in the financials and it is the experience of the firm or practitioner that the amount that is reasonably anticipated to be collected is at a lower rate, then a reserve should be charged against the work-in-process. For example, if accumulated work-in-process time charges for a law firm amount to $100,000 at the end of the fiscal period being reported upon, and the discount experience rate is four percent (4%), then there should be set up a reserve of $4,000 which would be charged against income at that date. The balance sheet and income statement would reflect work-in-process in the amount of $96,000.

The rate is arrived at by comparing fees collected with fees actually invoiced. There should be excluded from this calculation any fees invoiced to clients that have gone bankrupt or closed their doors, because this discount rate is based on write-downs from standard fees. Some firms call this their rate realization factor.

Bad debts due to worthlessness should be written off separately and should not influence the discount rate.

SUMMARY OF KEY POINTS

1. Prepare the trend analysis by comparing income statements over an extended time frame.
2. Look for major variances or changes from one period to another. This is a key to analysis.
3. Prepare monthly income statements. If information is not available, prepare an estimated flash statement utilizing as much actual information as possible, especially fees.
4. Be sure to use accrual-basis financials for management purposes.

6

How to Install Effective Management Controls to Maximize Profits

To maximize profits, your service business client should understand and monitor the cost relationships within its operations. One simple tool to create in this process of management control is the income statement, with all costs of doing business set forth as a percentage of the total. Naturally, each different type of service business should classify its operating expenses into certain general categories. For example, a radio or television station should group all expenses relating to each department, such as the Program Department, the Selling Department or the General & Administrative Department. Each department can be conceived of as a profit center. In the operation of a nursing home, as an illustration, there are four major categories of profit centers: Administrative, Dietary, Operating and Maintenance.

The financial statements should be prepared as simply as possible. However, the operating style of management will dictate the format that is most useful to management. You may find that most of your clients prefer comparative income statements. Some companies prefer to compare the current operations with prior periods. Other companies also require that comparative data be provided by measuring their own operations against information obtained from other companies in the same industry as well as comparing their own operations against a prior period. Many companies will compare actual monthly and year-to-date financials with budgeted monthly and year-to-date data. Prior-year comparisons should not be neglected.

Your client should watch certain expense percentages to see that they are normal. Furthermore, if these key percentages increase and exceed what your client considers to be the norm, then he must take corrective action to reduce the expense in order to maximize his profits. This type of action is judgmental.

TYPICAL APPLICATION OF KEY PERCENTAGES

Let us look at a specific situation. In typical real estate management, one of the key percentages to monitor is the relationship of repair and maintenance expense to income from rentals. As the building increases in age, this percentage will increase to a point where, on a cost-effective basis, it no longer makes sense to continue preventive maintenance and repair of certain equipment such as boilers, pumps or elevators. At that point, your client should decide to replace those aging capital assets. Finally, if the repair and maintenance percentage has been climbing each year and is approaching 10% per annum, your client may even decide that he would prefer to sell the real estate if he is unable to increase rental income adequately to recapture excessive operational costs.

The income statement alone is inadequate for management of real estate. If your client owns income-producing properties, the very least he must earn before depreciation is the amount that will satisfy the requirements to amortize the mortgage debt. If your real estate client shows a break-even on his income statement before depreciation, then he's in trouble. The problem arises because he must generate enough earnings to provide the cash flow necessary for debt service.

The reason your client should look at earnings before depreciation is that the depreciation expense may or may not be comparable to the amount required for debt service. Many real estate operators will use high rates of depreciation, resulting in an expense which is much greater than the amount needed to service the amortization of the mortgage. Therefore, for operational purposes, the number that counts is the one immediately preceding the depreciation expense, or, in other words, the income or loss from operations before depreciation expense. After the income statement is prepared, the income or loss from operations should be adjusted from an accrual basis to a cash basis to determine if the client is generating adequate cash to satisfy mortgage debt. Chapter 4 discusses this in detail.

Your real estate client should be able to forecast his expenses fairly closely at least one year in advance. Of course there will be unexpected items which will arise such as a repair. However, your client can use a percentage of his gross rent income and estimate that his repair expense will be that percentage. For example, if the gross rent is estimated to be $100,000 and your client estimates that his repair and maintenance expense should be 5%, then he can forecast a $5,000 repair and maintenance expense for the year. By forecasting his income statement for the year, your client will be able to see what he will earn from his operations and that he is able to amortize his mortgage debt. Furthermore, he should be able to ascertain the related income tax effect depending upon the structure that has been created for the operation.

STATEMENT OF OPERATIONS OF A RADIO STATION

Illustration #1 was utilized by a very successful local radio station. The statement of operations categorizes the various sources of revenue and expenses. However, depreciation expense is omitted from each department and segregated as a separate total expense. Although this corporation maintained its books and records on an accrual basis, management deemed it important to match revenues with related operating costs. Specifically, management was more interested in relating out-of-pocket operating expenses to broadcasting revenue than in relating total expenses to broadcasting revenue. Therefore, depreciation expense was not charged to each department but was segregated and set forth as an expense after operating income was determined.

In this illustration, during the three-month period, revenues in the amount of $238,144 were generated from the sale of station time, from which agency commissions were deducted in the amount of $28,194, leaving net broadcasting revenue in the amount of $209,950. Management incurred or spent 63.15% of this revenue for total operating expenses exclusive of depreciation charges. In each department, the major expense was salaries and related payroll taxes. In the sales department for example, 9.51% was expended for salaries and related payroll taxes. Obviously, a well-managed company should monitor this percentage continuously. If your radio or TV station client wants to establish a cost reduction program, payroll would be the first area to analyze because it is such a major portion of the total operation.

Now let us examine Kansas Missouri Radio Station Corp.'s statement of operations in Illustration #1.

COST REDUCTION PLANNING

If broadcasting revenue declines, you find that your client will object strongly to reducing sales' salaries on the theory that more sales effort is needed to increase broadcasting revenue. One simple solution is to find out if it is feasible to shift personnel, either part-time or full-time, from the general and administrative department (G and A) into an additional sales effort in order that broadcasting revenue may be increased. In many companies, the officers will shift their duties to aid the sales department. The president may decide to spend half of his time with the sales department, and therefore his salary should be

ILLUSTRATION #1

KANSAS MISSOURI RADIO CORP.

STATEMENT OF OPERATIONS

FOR THE THREE MONTHS ENDED SEPTEMBER 30, 19XX

(UNAUDITED)

	AMOUNT		PERCENT
BROADCASTING REVENUE— AM RADIO			
Local programs	$ 31,879		15.18
Local announcements	65,349		31.13
TOTAL LOCAL		$ 97,228	46.31
National programs	$ 3,300		1.57
National announcements	137,616		65.54
TOTAL NATIONAL		140,916	67.11
TOTAL SALE OF STATION TIME		$238,144	113.42
Less: Agency commissions		28,194	13.42
BROADCASTING REVENUE— AM RADIO		$209,950	100.00
EXPENSES			
Technical	$ 12,280		5.84
Program	47,134		22.45
Sales	33,822		16.11
General and administrative	39,344		18.75
TOTAL EXPENSES		132,580	63.15
OPERATING INCOME BEFORE DEPRECIATION		$ 77,370	36.85
DEPRECIATION EXPENSE		32,270	15.37
INCOME BEFORE INCOME TAXES		$ 45,100	21.48
INCOME TAXES		21,900	10.43
NET INCOME		$ 23,200	11.05

See Accompanying Notes

ILLUSTRATION #1 (continued)
KANSAS MISSOURI RADIO CORP.
DEPARTMENTAL EXPENSES
FOR THE THREE MONTHS ENDED SEPTEMBER 30, 19XX
(UNAUDITED)

	AMOUNT	PERCENT
TECHNICAL		
Salaries	$ 8,943	4.26
Payroll taxes	296	.14
Maintenance—buildings and grounds	544	.26
Maintenance—technical equipment	1,360	.65
Mobile unit	500	.24
Power and light	325	.15
Professional services	100	.04
Transmitter lines	212	.10
TOTAL TECHNICAL EXPENSES	$12,280	5.84
PROGRAM		
Salaries	$32,563	15.51
Payroll taxes	1,403	.67
Leasing equipment	42	.02
News services	2,637	1.26
Other	1,296	.62
Royalties and license fees	5,806	2.77
Talent	3,056	1.45
Tapes and discs	331	.15
TOTAL PROGRAM EXPENSES	$47,134	22.45
SALES		
Salaries	$19,322	9.20
Payroll taxes	649	.31
Advertising expenses	895	.43
National representative	3,718	1.77
Printing materials, photos	1,389	.66
Promotion	710	.34
Rent	1,032	.49
Salespersons' commissions	3,414	1.63
Salespersons' expenses	421	.20
Telephone	2,272	1.08
TOTAL SALES EXPENSES	$33,822	16.11

ILLUSTRATION #1 (continued)

KANSAS MISSOURI RADIO CORP.

DEPARTMENTAL EXPENSES

FOR THE THREE MONTHS ENDED SEPTEMBER 30, 19XX

(UNAUDITED)

	AMOUNT	PERCENT
GENERAL AND ADMINISTRATIVE		
Salaries	$19,342	9.21
Payroll taxes	917	.44
Collection expenses	25	.01
Dues and subscriptions	2,062	.98
Entertainment	1,061	.51
Insurance	938	.45
Leasing of office equipment	533	.25
Light and power	55	.02
Maintenance of office equipment	224	.11
Postage	504	.24
Professional services	2,307	1.10
Real and personal property taxes	672	.32
Rent	2,874	1.37
State sundry tax	83	.04
Supplies	971	.46
Telephone and telegraph	4,801	2.29
Travel and entertainment	721	.35
Other	1,254·	.60
TOTAL GENERAL AND ADMINISTRATIVE EXPENSES	$39,344	18.75

allocated between sales and G and A. Many companies with declining broadcasting revenue will hire additional salespersons, considering that the additional cost will be an investment to recapture the lost revenue. While a company is going through this process of stimulating sales to improve revenue, it should be simultaneously reviewing its expenses to see what percentages are out of line and which should be reduced accordingly. For example, one such company told its salespersons to entertain at cheaper restaurants. Another company bought cheaper automobiles for its personnel.

HOW TO KEEP TABS ON A BUSINESS BY USING COMPARATIVE FINANCIAL DATA

Management of Kansas Missouri Radio Corp. should compare the statement of operations for the three months ended September 30 with the prior quarters, that is, the three months ended June 30th and the three months ended September 30, of the prior year. The historical data for the prior quarter and the year-ago-same-quarter should be compared on a percentage basis to see that the percentages are still in line. Of course, certain costs and expenses will be controllable and others will not be controllable. However, each expense should be scrutinized.

Another approach that your client in the radio station business can take is to compare operating data with similar data from other companies. There are many sources of such data in the broadcasting industry such as the Federal Communications Commission, The Robert Morris Associates, various trade magazines, and publicly owned radio stations which must publish their financial statements.

When your client compares the operations of his corporation to other companies in the same industry, he must be careful to recognize that there may be peculiarities which may not apply to his operation. For example, in a survey of a number of AM radio stations during the year 1973, it was determined that officers' salaries averaged approximately 12% of the broadcasting revenue. This percentage seems to be unusually high, unless the stations in the group were very small and all other payroll was relatively minor in comparison to the officers' payroll. In Illustration #1 for the Kansas Missouri Radio Corp., salaries in all departments totalled 38.17% of broadcasting revenues.

In analyzing the financial statements of Kansas Missouri Radio Corp., if the officers wondered why their salary percentage was so much lower, you might indicate that the apparently excessive percentage may be due to the fact that in some small radio stations, the officers attempt to distribute dividends to themselves in the form of additional salaries and that therefore the percentages were not in line with Kansas Missouri Radio Corp.'s percentages. To bear out this contention, the same survey in the AM radio station industry indicated a pre-tax profit of approximately 8%, whereas the Kansas Missouri Radio Corp. for the three months ended September 30 had a pre-tax profit of 21.48%. Chapter 8 will present this problem of income tax planning and the problems of officers' salaries. If you are seeking guidelines regarding your clients' salaries, turn to Chapter 8.

PROFIT CONTROL OF PERSONAL SERVICE BUSINESSES

You may find, in your initial audit of a personal service business, that the books and records are maintained on a cash basis. It is obvious that the proper way to analyze a personal service business is to maintain the books on an accrual basis. Your client may complain that if you require that he accrue income, he would also be required to pay the related income taxes. You should answer his objection by pointing out that it is perfectly proper to keep the books on a cash basis, but, for financial statement purposes, the statements should be converted to an accrual basis.

Some personal service businesses readily lend themselves to a cash basis. For example, bowling alley operators and barbershops operate strictly on a cash basis and no accrual of income is required. However, these are exceptions rather than the rule. Most personal service businesses extend credit: doctors and dentists to patients; attorneys, accountants and architects to clients; brokers to customers, and so on.

Unless you insist that your client prepare financials based on the accrual method of accounting, you will not be able to analyze his business for him in a meaningful manner. Sometimes an argument will be raised by the client that the accruals at the beginning of a period will offset the accruals at the end of a period. No one really knows, and the only thing that this can lead to is a distortion of both income and expenses. If you are concerned about the tax problems, please turn at this point to Chapter 8.

Your client in the personal service business must be able to earn a profit (although it is difficult for some doctors to think of themselves as being in business) after deducting all expenses.

Expenses should fall into three categories:

1. Operating expenses
2. Salary or salaries of the one rendering the personal service
3. A theoretical expense which must be computed, consisting of a fair rate of return on the investment made by your client

HOW TO SET UP RATE-OF-RETURN GUIDEPOSTS

It should be easy for you to identify all of the operating expenses. Furthermore, you should determine an adequate rate-of-return level for your client. You should point out to your client that he is entitled to a fair return on his investment. For example, a dentist will have a substantial investment in fixed assets as well as in receivables. If the client, the dentist, were able to take all these monies and invest them in a savings bank, the bank would pay interest on this investment. It probably will be necessary to explain to your client that he is entitled to earn a fair rate of return from this investment as it relates to his personal service business. If the salary that he draws and the profit that he earns do not include a fair return on his investment, then your client's business is not being run properly.

The question then arises, "What is a fair return?" The easiest way to approach a solution to this question is to say, "What would be a fair return if the monies were invested in a savings bank?" Whatever that percentage is, it would certainly be a conservative return. In fact, your client may not be satisfied with such a low rate of return on his investment. Therefore, the answer becomes judgmental, depending upon the rate of return that your client seeks on the capital invested in his personal service business. Assuming that your client is satisfied with an 8% return on his investment, if your client has $40,000 invested in equipment and other assets, then he should try to obtain $3,200 from his business over and above any salary and profit.

Let's look at an illustration for your dentist client, using the following set of facts:

Operating expenses	$45,000
Salary of client	60,000
Capital investment	40,000
Return-on-investment	3,200

Now let's see what his practice looks like in Illustration #2.

ILLUSTRATION #2

DR. PETER WILLIAMS

INCOME STATEMENT

FOR THE YEAR ENDED 19XX

		ACCRUAL BASIS	CASH BASIS
Fee Income		$121,700	$106,300
Operating Expenses		45,000	45,000
Net Income		$ 76,700	$ 61,300
	OR		
Fee Income		$121,700	$106,300
Operating Expenses	$45,000		
Salary of Client	60,000		
Total		105,000	105,000
Net Income		$ 16,700	$ 1,300
	OR		
Fee Income		$121,700	$106,300
Operating Expenses	$45,000		
Salary of Client	60,000		
Return-on-Investment Expense	3,200		
Total		108,200	105,000
Net Income		$ 13,500	$ 1,300

In this illustration, your client grossed fees of $121,700 and it cost him $45,000 to do this business. Therefore he was left with a net income of $76,700. He believes he is entitled to a salary of $60,000 and a return-on-investment of $3,200. Thus he earned a net income of $13,500.

The preceding illustration has been prepared both on an accrual basis and a cash basis. This should be done so that the client will understand that, for income tax purposes, he will report a net income of $61,300, whereas his actual earnings exceeded that amount by $15,400. It is up to you to explain to him that he must look at his practice from the viewpoint of an accrual basis to really know what his true income was.

An easier way to explain this is to say that each day he works, he earns certain gross fees. At the end of a week, month, or year, those fees constitute his fee income. In other words, his fee income is not determined by the amount he has collected, but rather by the work that he has produced. His operating expenses should be related to the work he is doing and to the fees he has produced, not to the fees that he has collected. In fact, your dentist client may have to borrow if his collections from his patients fall short during any given period. Older, established practitioners try to prevent borrowing by keeping an adequate cash balance available for such shortfalls in fee collections.

Your client may try to argue with you and contend that he may not collect all of these fees and therefore his financials should be on a cash basis rather than accrual. The best response is to sit down with your client and have him estimate, on an annual basis, the amount that he may not collect. Then, in preparing his accrual-basis financials, you should set forth as an expense an "allowance for uncollectible accounts" based on his prior years' experience. All operating expenses have been grouped into the $45,000 figure in this illustration, including depreciation expense and the "allowance for uncollectible accounts" expense.

One dentist client of mine sits down at the end of each workday and computes his net income for the day after adding up all of the fees that he has earned and deducting his estimated daily operating expenses.

In Illustration #2, Dr. Peter Williams grossed $121,700. His net income of $76,000, divided by 250 workdays, shows a net income for each workday in the amount of $306.80 per day. On a cash basis, his income was $245.20 per day, or approximately 25% less than his true net income per day on an accrual basis. His operating expenses of $45,000 amounted to $180 per workday. Each workday therefore cost Dr. Williams $180. Any fees earned in excess of that amount represent net earnings for that day. Any fees earned below $180 in one workday represent a loss for that day.

	Fees Earned	Operating Expenses	Earnings or (Loss)
Monday	$600	$180	$ 420
Tuesday	310	180	130
Wednesday	340	180	160
Thursday	175	180	(5)
Friday	495	180	315
Week	$1,920	$900	$1,020

It is important to keep in mind that the $180 per workday cost is an approximation based on historical costs. One way to make yourself valuable to your client is to be sure that the overhead or "nut" is recalculated at least monthly. Dr. Williams' "nut," based on a $45,000 annual overhead expense, is $3,750 per month. His out-of-pocket expenses are lower because depreciation is a non-cash expense as well as the allowance for uncollectible accounts. Be sure that all expenses are included in the "nut," especially those expenses which accrue throughout the year. For example, Dr. Williams' nurse gets a Christmas bonus of $1,200. He may think of this as a December item, but you should explain to him that you have included $100 per month as an expense. She is earning this bonus at that rate each month. Of course, in December, Dr. Williams has to be prepared to pay out the $1,200 bonus. As the year progresses, he may want to accumulate the cash needed to make this payment in December. Many professionals set aside funds each month into separate bank accounts for Christmas bonuses or other large routine payments such as withdrawals for income taxes, payments for equipment, repayment of loans and other unusual items.

PERCENTAGE CONTROLS

Let's look at Illustration #2 from the viewpoint of percentage controls.

Fee Income	$121,700	100.00%
Operating Expenses	45,000	36.98
Net Income	$ 76,700	63.02%

This simple analysis shows that Dr. Williams earns approximately sixty-three cents for every dollar he grosses in fees. Put another way, Dr. Williams spends about thirty-seven cents each time he grosses one dollar. That percentage relationship is significant. Every single element of expense should be broken down by percentage, including salaries of nurses, payroll taxes, insurance, rent, telephone, travel, stationery, collection cost, professional services, and so on. These percentages should be evaluated monthly. Two doctors sharing the rent in one office will drop the percentage in half and your client will earn a greater net income. Many doctors will share as many operating costs as feasible. These include offices, nurses, office equipment and laboratory equipment. Even when only one office is rented for the doctors' use, it may be possible to schedule patients' office hours on some sort of a staggered basis such as mornings for one doctor and afternoons for another doctor. Shared facilities are often set up as medical clinics.

HOW TO USE STATISTICAL DATA TO MEASURE COSTS

Each service business employs certain statistical data to measure cost and to maximize profits. These data are related to the particular business. For example, in real estate management, the statistical data are related to the square footage available for rental. In the coin-operated laundry vending business, it is the cost to service one vending machine (i.e., one piece of equipment). In nursing homes, the overall percentage of occupancy is determined based on a ratio of actual patient days to the maximum number of patient days (based on bed complement) during any given period of time. Furthermore, in nursing homes, for example, each department is quantitatively measured. Customary measurements in the operation of any nursing home department are: (1) the volume of work produced or rendered by that department expressed in units of service, (2) the dollar amount of labor required for the rendering of such service, (3) the amount of labor expressed in the number of employee-days or employee-hours required to render such services.

NURSING HOME STATISTICS

Let's take a look at the statistical information required for each of the departments in a typical nursing home.

Administration and General

The unit of service to be determined for this department is the total number of patient admissions, discharges, and the cumulative census for the period.

Dietary

The unit of service for the dietary department should be a "served meal." Where there are pay cafeterias or other similar pay dining areas, the "served meal" should not be utilized and sales dollars would be gathered.

The number of "served meals" should be further sub-classified according to meals served patients, nursing home employees, special nurses, and others.

Housekeeping Department

Records should be kept of housekeeping employee-days or employee-hours of service rendered to each of the departments within the nursing home.

Laundry Department

The unit of service for the laundry department should be pounds or pieces of laundry processed. This information should also be classified by nursing home departments, nursing units, or classes of patients served, as well as personal work for nursing home personnel.

Patient Care

Professional care of patients should be classified and recorded by the nature of service performed and the amount of such service for each class. These categories would fall into the following departmental charges:

a. Nursing Service
b. Oxygen Services and Equipment Rental
c. Laboratory
d. Medical and Surgical Supply Charges
e. Pharmacy
f. Private Room Charges
g. Medical Records
h. X-ray
i. Occupational Therapy
j. Physical Therapy
k. Recreational Activities
l. Social Services
m. Operation of Records and Forms
n. Special Transportation
o. Religious
p. Dental Care

Statistics should be kept in other areas such as the number of employees who live in, classified according to the department in which they are employed. Personnel assigned to the repair and maintenance of buildings, equipment and grounds should be measured in terms of employee-hours of service rendered. This too should be further sub-classified according to the nature of the work performed. Materials used by these personnel in making repairs or replacements should be charged to each of the departments.

Nursing Service

Let's take a look at the type of information required by a good administration to determine the relationship of nursing services to the patient census and the costs of such services. In this department, a record should be kept of the actual number of hours or days of nursing service rendered. This service should be categorized as follows:

1. Supervisors and Head Nurses
2. General Duty—Registered Nurses
3. Practical Nurses
4. Nurses Aides
5. Nursing Attendants
6. Orderlies
7. Private Duty Nurses
8. Others

Furthermore, the nursing statistics should also be classified on the basis of the patients' financial relationships to the nursing home. Patients' financial relationships are usually classified as:

1. Private
2. Contractual
3. Medicare
4. Medicaid
5. MAA
6. Other

Each of the departmental categories enumerated on page 156 should be analyzed and classified by the patient's financial relationship with the nursing home. The total costs charged to each of the departments should be segregated.

Now let's look at the typical nursing home and see the way maintenance department expenses are broken down and set forth in the financials. (See Illustration #3.)

The key to controlling maintenance expenses is to watch each month the cumulative costs as they compare with the column headed "Budget—This Year." As the year progresses it should be apparent to the administrator and to the accountants or auditors that the monthly expenses should be increasing at a rate such that the budget is not exceeded when the year ends. Prior years' comparative expenses are informative because certain months may contain unusually large costs due to cyclical factors. For example, during the winter months, the payroll and related fringe costs for gardeners should decline substantially. The budgeted amount may only be for a six-month period, depending upon the geographical location of the nursing home. In warmer climates, gardening payroll will not vary significantly from month to month.

Some administrators may desire a different format for the financials. As the accountant, you should review the various possibilities. For example, you may suggest additional columns for variances between budget and actual. Many administrators prefer this format because they can utilize the management-by-exception approach to financial statement analysis. Other administrators like an additional column to compare the prior year's budget with current financials.

When you install adequate financials and controls, it will be necessary for you to review the information that is sought by your client. Furthermore, based on the client's organization, you should be prepared to recommend the format that is paticularly applicable and suitable.

INTERNAL CONTROLS

The most essential controls that you will be required to set up for your client are proper internal controls over income and expenses. If your service business client receives cash, then you will be called upon to install a system which ensures that all of the cash is collected and deposited. Each system of internal controls should be tailored to the business.

ILLUSTRATION #3

	Month of September 19X7	Cumulative This Year	Budget This Year	Month of September 19X6	Cumulative Last Year
	(1)	(2)	(3)	(4)	(5)
MAINTENANCE EXPENSES	$	$	$	$	$
Contract Services					
Elevators					
Exterminators					
Gardening					
Patrol Service					
Watchman Service					
Other					
Decorating					
Furniture and Furnishings					
Carpets					
Draperies					
Furniture					
Ground Materials and Equipment					
Insurance					
Fire					
Furniture and Furnishings					
Liability					
Property					
Other					
Payroll and Fringes					
Superintendent					
Maintenance Men					
Gardeners					
Watchmen					
Employee Benefits					
Payroll Taxes					
Repairs and General Maintenance					
Vehicles					
Depreciation					
Gasoline					
Repairs					
Rentals					
Other					
Total Maintenance Expenses					

Even if no actual cash is received and all payments to your client are in the form of checks, internal control systems are important. For example, as the accountant for a radio station, you should compare the station "log" of programs broadcast with the related time contracts and sales invoices.

On one audit of a radio station, we found that spot announcements were broadcast from the "log," but we could find no billings for these particular advertisements. The result of our examination was that we uncovered the fact that the radio station manager was using an automobile for which he had bartered time on the air. He was diverting the advertising income into his own pocket. The owners of this station lived in another state and knew nothing about this scheme.

SUMMARY OF KEY POINTS

Now, let's wrap up the essence of what we talked about in this chapter.

First, the income statement should be comparative with the prior year both in dollars and percentages. All costs of doing business should be expressed as a percent of total.

Second, cost-reduction programs should concentrate on the areas of highest percent of cost of total operation, usually payroll and related fringe costs.

Third, if key costs increase and exceed budgets or guidelines, corrective action should be recommended to your client.

Fourth, compare your client's business to others in the same industry. Prepare a supplementary report explaining variances to management and suggest possible solutions in problem areas.

Fifth, convince your client that, for purposes of accounting and improved management control, he maintain his financials on the accrual basis, not on a cash basis.

Sixth, be sure that internal controls over income and expenses provide a checking system so that income is tied to proper documentation which can be monitored separately. Expenses should be properly budgeted and approved by someone in authority.

Finally, check to see that your client is earning a fair rate of return on his investment (ROI).

7

How to Function as Your
Client's Independent Treasurer

As the independent public accountant for a service business, you may perform the function of treasurer. Many accountants are not aware of the fact that they are indeed performing this function. For example, when your client looks to you to help him solve his financial problems, you are performing the function of an independent treasurer.

From the inception of the service business, and as it continues to grow, financing will from time to time become a problem. One of your tasks will be to recognize the problem as it arises and to help solve the problem. Before you can help your client in tapping sources of funds, you should ascertain how much is needed and why. One of the primary tasks you will have when you are retained by a client who is organizing a business is to help ascertain how much initial investment will be needed.

The best approach is to sit down with your client and develop a "business plan." The plan should spell out the goals of the client and how your client intends to arrive at those goals. The plan should include a financial forecast consisting of a forecast of earnings as well as assets to be employed in the business. In most small service businesses, financing is provided by the initial investment, trade and bank payables, and by generation of internal earnings. However, the successful business may grow so rapidly that earnings may not be adequate to pay for the increases in assets required in the business. For example, in personal service businesses such as advertising agencies, law firms or brokerage companies, a successful operation may cause a substantial increase in receivables. Your client may be very profitable, and be faced with inadequate cash.

HOW TO DEVELOP A BUSINESS PLAN

The thing to do is to try to anticipate by planning. You can develop, with your client, a business plan which essentially may be divided into two phases:

—Development of a profit plan to determine earnings.
—Development of a capital plan to determine the assets needed for the implementation of the profit plan.

Let's be more specific. A profit plan is simply a forecast of the income statement. A capital plan is simply a forecast of the balance sheet.

To help your client plan, you should ask the following questions:

1. What does your client anticipate in the way of revenues over the next twelve-month period? This should be done on a month-by-month basis. No matter how hard your client may resist this type of planning, it is imperative that you explain the reasons for such a forecast. By forecasting revenues and then forecasting related expenses and costs, you will arrive at a forecast of earnings. When this is done on a month-by-month basis, there may be periods in which a loss can be anticipated. Many clients may need a plan prepared on a weekly basis.

2. What costs and expenses will be incurred to generate the revenues anticipated over the twelve-month period of the business plan?

3. At this point you may want to turn to the end of Chapter 2. It is suggested that you ask the stated "key questions" in order to set up a balance sheet plan.

4. Go back to Chapter 3 which explains cash flow and how to forecast business needs.

SIZING UP SOURCES OF AVAILABLE FUNDS

After you have assisted your client in developing a "business plan," you should look at the sources of funds available as well as the needs for the funds.

Sources of funds fall into four categories:

a. Private
b. Trade
c. Institutional
d. Governmental

Look at each of these sources and determine when to use each.

a. Private Sources

The safest way to inject new funds into your client's business is from private sources, depending upon availability, the amount of funds required and the length of time that the business will need to have the funds. Four private sources may be available: (1) personal savings of the client, (2) family funds from relatives, (3) funds from friends of the client, and (4) "private placement" funds available from outsiders interested in loaning money or making an investment in the business. Sometimes your client's attorney may suggest a "private placement" source of funds. Here is an illustration of a private source: I was once approached by my dentist, who said that he wanted to make a loan or make an investment in any small private corporation. This particular dentist had investments in marketable securities and real estate, had money in savings institutions and was desirous of putting funds into a privately owned company.

The source of funds should usually bear a relationship to the amount of the funds and to the time that your client will need to retain the funds in the business. For example, if in developing a business plan, it is ascertained that during a short time frame there will be needed a small amount of money which could be available from the savings account of your client, it would be preferable for the client to withdraw his funds on a temporary basis from his personal savings. You could have him make a short loan to his business. On an arm's length basis, the business would pay him interest in connection with the funds loaned. However, it may well be that the funds are needed permanently or at least you may ascertain that for several years in the future the business will not be able to repay your client. If your client has excess cash which can be loaned to the business for several years without going to strangers or financial institutions, it would be safer from the viewpoint that "outside" sources would want protection or guarantees of their funds. If your client makes a short-term or long-term loan to his own business, he will not be overly concerned with collateral. Furthermore, in the event that the business is unable to amortize its debt to your client in accordance with the plan (which debt should be evidenced by a note bearing a reasonable rate of interest) there will be no problem stretching out the amortization period or even declaring a hiatus on the repayment. However, non-private lenders or investors may not be so understanding.

One word of caution: Some accounting firms find that it is very profitable to make loans to clients. If you do this, not only will you impair your independence, but you may wind up antagonizing your client. We have seen another accounting firm lose its client and have to sue to recover the loan. If you, as the independent treasurer, believe that your client is entitled to financing, you should be able to help obtain this financing from other sources.

b. Trade Sources

Financing may be obtained from trade sources in many ways other than usual trade credit. Short-term money may be available by extending the customary trade payment period. You may arrange with your client to meet one or more large creditors to explain your client's needs for a longer time to pay. If your client has developed good relationships, this type of arrangement may provide the additional financing necessary. In many types of service businesses, your client's vendors will provide long-term financing which may be more advantageous than bank financing because the vendor is also desirous of making the sale.

Personal service businesses sometimes have the opportunity to obtain funds from the recipient of the service which helps in the financing of their business. For example, law firms routinely ask for retainer fees from clients before performing their services. Law firms with significant retainer practices may find their cash flow problems minimized. Schools will require payments at the beginning of the academic year. Travel agencies will require deposits. Many other personal service businesses will progress bill and collect in installments for services rendered, either as the service is performed or in advance of services rendered.

In most service businesses, trade credit is not a major financing source because of the nature of the business. Typically, service businesses are labor intensive—payroll and related expenses are usually the largest single element of operational costs. Therefore, trade credit becomes secondary. Your service business client must meet its payroll on time, and for this expense no credit is available except from financial institutions or governmental agencies. Of course, payroll can be paid over longer time frames, extending from weekly to every other week, twice a month, or even monthly. However, if your client pays its employees weekly and wants to shift to every other week, your client may find it will have to finance its employees between paydays until they are able to adjust to the change. It may very well be that in certain service businesses and in certain geographic areas, employees may simply be unwilling or unable to shift from a weekly payroll.

c. Institutional Sources

Let's look at the various institutional sources of credit and how they operate. Credit grantors are primarily concerned with the ability of your client to repay. Keep in mind that the grantor of credit will be looking at your client's balance sheet with a view towards potential liquidation of assets. In other words, what collateral can your client provide to assure the grantor of the credit that he will get his money back?

Service businesses are essentially very different than other types of businesses in the sense that they are unable to provide an inventory as collateral for a loan like the typical manufacturer or retailer or wholesaler. However, most of the usual institutional sources are available to service companies. These include banks, insurance companies, investment banking firms or underwriters, savings and loan associations, factors, finance companies, small business investment companies (SBIC) and leasing companies.

How Will a Bank Look at Your Client?

To be your client's independent treasurer, you really have to know to which source of funds to go and why. Each of these different institutions approaches financing from a different perspective. Commercial banks traditionally seek to loan short-term funds. Therefore, if your client has short-term needs (by "short-term" we mean a twelve-month period), you should approach a commercial bank. For example, if you have a client that owns a bowling alley, which is usually a very seasonal business, during certain times of the year there may be a negative cash position which will be cured when the season changes. This type of situation is natural for a commercial bank loan because, as the business cycle changes, the funds will be adequate to repay the loan. If your client is operating sucessfully and has this type of need, a commercial bank will often require no more than your client's personal guarantee on the loan and will require no collateral by his business.

Many commercial banks have branched out into other areas of financing. Many of them, for example, are granting longer loans than the traditional one-year loan. Many of them have also gone into financing and factoring so that they are in direct competition with the factoring companies. If your local bank provides many other kinds of services in addition to the normal and customary short-term loans, it would be advantageous for you to inquire in order to get competitive information for your client.

Insurance Loans

Insurance companies represent a source of long-term financing. In fact, insurance companies traditionally will not make short-term loans the way the banks do. Futhermore, many insurance companies will not make long-term loans unless there is substantial collateral to secure the loan, such as real estate, or significant office equipment such as computers, and so on.

Savings and Loan Associations

Savings and loan associations are another source of credit. They are usually restricted to long-term mortgage financing of real estate, and therefore do not represent much of an opportunity if there is no real estate involved in the operation of your client's service business.

Underwriters

Investment bankers or underwriters may be a source of long-term funds for your service business client. However, most underwriters are primarily interested in selling securities to the investing public or possibly obtaining a piece of your client's business for themselves. Investment bankers have operated to finance service businesses in all areas other than personal services. However, several years ago, certain personal service businesses such as advertising agencies and securities brokers began to sell their securities to the public.

Factors, Finance and Leasing Companies

Factors, finance companies, and leasing companies are good sources of funds for your client, if your client has the right kind of collateral. These companies generally charge higher rates of interest than banks traditionally charge. However, as long as your client continues to operate profitably and continues to provide collateral to satisfy the factor, finance company or leasing company, the substitution of one piece of collateral for another provides a continuous flow of funds into the business. For example, as your service client generates trade accounts receivable, a factoring company will advance funds to your client against the receivables. The amount usually advanced by the factor is a percentage of the gross receivable. When your client collects the total receivable from his client or customer, he remits the advance to the factor. However, by that time he has generated an additional receivable against which he has received another advance from the factor. In effect, the funds rotate or revolve from the factor continuously, as long as the business continues to operate profitably, and in effect there is no repayment or amortization. Of course, if your service business client buys a large fixed asset which is leased, then the customary leasing arrangement would provide for a long-term amortization of the funds borrowed from the leasing company.

This overview of the various institutional sources of financing does not take into account specific variations from institution to institution. To do your job well you should be acquainted with the parameters that various local institutions use in judging loans and with the nature of the loans that they seek. For example, a large financing or factoring company may not be interested in making a secured loan to your client if the loan is too small, say $100,000 or less. A giant insurance company, however, might be interested in making a long-term loan of a much smaller size. Therefore, it becomes incumbent upon you to have a preliminary dialogue with various institutions to find out the parameters of each. Furthermore, parameters change from time to time so you should keep current in order to do your job as your client's independent treasurer.

Educating the Lender

Probably the most difficult job that you will have in seeking financing is the education of the potential lender as to the real nature of your client's business. For example, commercial bankers generally tend to look for working capital. One of the parameters of most commercial banks for short-term financing is the amount of working capital the company will have. Most commercial banks prefer not to make a short-term loan in excess of the working capital. Therefore, you will have to explain to the banker that your client, because of the nature of the business, has no true working capital and that the loan will have to be based on other criteria. It should be very clear to you that commercial bankers, like any other lenders, are primarily interested in the ability of your client to repay. As long as your client is operating a successful business and you can demonstrate that with adequate financials, documentation, and projections, you should have no problem in securing financing for your client. Be prepared that the commercial banker may not like the way your client's balance sheet looks just because he is in a service business.

SBIC Capital

If your client is mainly interested in finding an additional investor in his business, a long-term lender, or a combination of both, then you might find it advisable to turn to a small business investment company (SBIC). These are private companies, licensed by the Small Business Administration of the United States Government, whose primary function is to make long-term loans or investments in small businesses.

Your client will typically have to pay a higher price for his money from an SBIC than from other long-term lending sources such as insurance companies. However, where an insurance company may be reluctant to make a loan, the SBIC is normally prepared to take a higher risk. In many cases the SBIC will require that your client grant the SBIC an option to purchase securities of your client, possibly with a "put" back to your client in the event that your client does not desire to sell its securities to the public. This type of option of course raises the cost of borrowing money even further. Despite the high cost of doing business with an SBIC, many successful companies have utilized SBIC funds where there was really no other source of long-term money available.

d. Governmental Sources of Funds

In almost every level of government there are sources of funds available for the privately owned corporation. The primary source of funds from the Federal Government is the Small Business Administration. Funds are also available from various state governments, city governments, regional agencies, county governments and other local financing agencies created especially for that purpose.

The Small Business Administration may be a source of funds for your client in the event that your client can prove that no other source of funds is available. The SBA may make a direct loan to your client, or working with a bank may guarantee 90% of the loan that the bank makes. In either case, these loans are always long-term loans at very favorable rates of interest.

Each state, city, town, county, and other local financing authority has different rules and regulations regarding financing. Some local governmental agencies will make direct loans. Other local governmental agencies prefer to guarantee local bank loans. In any case, the best approach here is to consult with your local authorities, whether they be the mayor, the governor's office or some other local governmental authority. You can be advised as to where and how to apply and what information the local governmental agency is seeking in connection with the loan. **One word of caution:** Obtaining funds from any governmental agency, SBA or local, you will find is a much longer process than obtaining funds from an institutional source such as a bank or an insurance company. When you are seeking funds from a bank for your client you can get a fairly rapid yes or no. However, if you are seeking funds for your client from the Small Business Administration, it will surely be several months before you can get a yes or a no, and then more time will elapse until you will be able to close the loan.

One good way to approach government funding authorities we have found is through counsel. Usually your client's attorney will be able to assist in dealing with governmental agencies, or he can at least make suggestions as to how to go about obtaining the funds.

MATCHING THE RIGHT FUND SOURCE TO THE NEED OF THE BUSINESS

Your client's need for funds will fall into one of two categories: (1) short-term temporary or seasonal needs to be repaid within a year or (2) long-term to be either permanently invested in the business or to be repaid over many, many years. It is very important that you go to the right source, depending upon the length of time your client will need the funds. From the inception of the business, and as it grows, it will be important for you to measure your client's need. Therefore, you should match up the source of funds with the appropriate time length that your client needs the money. Even after you have done this, it will be important to monitor the amortization of the loan, for you may find that your client's earnings are inadequate to amortize the loan even on a short-term basis. Conversely, you may find that your client's earnings are so great that more than enough cash is generated from earnings. Then the loan can be repaid in a shorter period of time than originally forecast.

Personal funds are usually the best sources for the original capitalization of the business. In other words, you should persuade your client to invest his own funds or funds from his family when he starts his business. You should explain to your client that whoever makes an investment in his business will require a degree of control related to that investment. Therefore, if your client is able to set up his own business with his own monies, he will be in full control of the business. Furthermore, you will have helped him eliminate a need for amortization of funds. Even though you may be able to obtain bank loans for your client when he begins his business, it may be quite difficult for him to amortize these loans out of earnings. You may find, after a period of time, that you have actually done him a disservice by arranging for the wrong type of financing. If you are called in to advise a company that is about to be created, and you find at the end of your analysis that your client does not have enough of his own funds to invest in his company, then he probably should wait to accumulate enough initial capital. It may be your difficult duty to advise him not to begin but to wait or to continue to seek additional initial capital. You should explain at this point that most businesses fail within a year or two after they have been created because the owners have not arranged for adequate initial financing. You should explain to your client that the start-up phase of any business will run into unusual costs and expenses which may deplete the initial funds. Many good businesses have failed during either the first or second year of operation because the business had simply run out of cash. This can happen to a business that is very profitable as well as to a business that is only marginal. For example, an aggressive young attorney who opened his own office found that he had a lot of work but he had trouble collecting his receivables. His law practice was successful and growing, but his receivables were going up at such a rate that it was difficult for him to sustain his personal life. In this case, there was no dearth of clients and the practice was profitable. The real question that had to be determined was, "When would the cash flow be positive to sustain the practice?"

RECOGNIZE THE RIGHT NEEDS

Once the business is off and running, you will encounter both short-term and long-term financing needs. Short-term needs such as a temporary buildup in accounts receivable should be financed from temporary sources such as bank loans. Long-term financing for fixed assets should come from long-term sources such as insurance companies. Intermediate-type loans such as two- or three-year loans are also usually commercial bank loans. Many commercial banks will make loans for even as long as five years to small businesses. Another common way to finance fixed assets such as equipment is through the medium of a lease financing arrangement. Leasing companies, and even banks, will be pleased to make arrangements of this sort. Typically, in a lease financing arrangement, your client must be prepared to put up a certain amount of capital and the balance will be financed. For example, if your client wants to buy or lease a $75,000 mini-computer, he may be able to obtain a lease which will arrange for financing of $67,500. The balance of the money should come from the business in the amount of $7,500. These leases can be arranged in such a way that, at the end of the lease period, your client will own the fixed asset without any additional payments or with some nominal payment.

PURCHASE FINANCING OF EXISTING BUSINESSES

If your client plans to purchase an existing business, he may be able to make an arrangement whereby the seller of the business will provide the financing. This is usually done by having your client make a substantial down payment and the balance of the purchase price paid out over an extended period of time, with the seller taking back some sort of lien on the business. Of course, your client will be required to pay interest as well as amortization on this debt, and it will be incumbent upon you to prepare for your client a forecast as to whether or not he will be able to amortize the debt. Here we return to the business plan: What are the anticipated revenues and expenses and what does your client anticipate earning? The earnings must be sufficient for your client to repay the seller of the business as well as pay interest on the obligation to the seller. Of course the more your client invests, the smaller his obligation and the easier to sustain the debt loan.

Business acquisition loans are also available from financial institutions such as finance companies, banks, and others.

The SBA and local governments are quite anxious to assist the small businessman at the inception of a business or in connection with acquisition of a business. You may very well suggest that your client approach the Small Business Administration or some local governmental agency to arrange for long-term financing. Financing of this sort usually runs between five and ten years at very favorable interest rates, depending upon the situation. Many local governments have set up financing agencies to attract businesses or to induce businesses to remain in a specific geographic area. Here again, local counsel selected by your client could be of service. You should not hesitate to approach local government directly, whether it be the office of the mayor or the office of the governor, to seek governmental assistance.

HOW TO SET UP PERFORMANCE
MEASURING DEVICES—A RECAP

Every type of service business uses special performance measuring devices that help to evaluate the business. It's really up to you to ascertain which statistics will be most meaningful to your client in evaluating and controlling his business.

The statistics are always related to the primary goals of the client. If your client is in the vending machine business, as an illustration, he would be interested in "per-machine" data. For example, with 1,000 machines in operation in different locations he would need to know:

a. gross income per machine
b. operating costs per machine
c. commission expense per machine
d. net income per machine
e. net income per employee
f. revenue-producing fixed assets per employee.

Machines are usually grouped by location. Gross income per machine in a given location may be compared with the average gross income computed for all machines. There will be seasonal as well as locational variations. Your client should set up budgets for each of his per-machine statistics. Then he could compare gross income per machine with budgeted gross income per machine. In the event that the actual per-machine gross income does not reach the budgeted gross income per machine, he will be forced to take action. If budgeted operating costs per machine are exceeded by actual operating costs per machine, he may be forced to shift locations or take other corrective actions such as reducing commissions.

In many service businesses there are trade or professional associations which publish operating statistical data. Your client can use this data as a basis of comparison with his company's statistical data.

The hotel and motel industry uses information such as occupancy rate which also varies geographically. Each hotel has a break-even rate of occupancy in its room rental operations. Budgeted net income per room should be compared with actual net income per room.

Chapter 6, "How to Install Effective Management Controls to Maximize Profits," discussed how to use statistical data to measure costs, especially in nursing homes. Essentially, you set up performance-measuring devices by analyzing your client's business goals to determine what is significant. If time is a factor, then it must be measured. Standards should be set up against which actual performance is measured. For instance, in a law firm it is important to measure fees realized. This is computed by dividing actual fees collected by fees charged. The resulting percentage is the "realization percentage." Some firms determine an annual "realization percentage," then, in forecasting receipts and preparing budgets, this percentage is used. For example, if a law firm budgets $1,200,000 in revenues during the next fiscal year and had a prior "realization percentage" in the last fiscal year of 90%, their estimated receipts are forecast at $1,080,000. Each partner's performance is evaluated by many factors, one of which is fee realization.

Judgment is essential in setting up performance measuring devices. What may be practical for one service business may be impractical for another. The key question to ask is, "How can it be useful to help your client control his business efficiently?"

TO SUM UP

Help your client develop a business plan. Size up sources of available funds. Match your client's needs with the right fund source.

What is different about service businesses? They have no product to sell. Service businesses usually sell time—directly, like a lawyer or architect, or indirectly, like a truck rental company. They do, however, need business plans.

Financial statements of service businesses are different. Balance sheets cannot be classified. Statements of changes in financial position are much more meaningful. Budgets are important control tools. Cash control and measurement are as important as income measurement. People are a significant ingredient in the service business. Your client should know how to motivate and encourage his organization with a well-designed financial package.

Analyze your client's business so that you can become his independent treasurer. His business will grow, and your practice will grow with him.

8

Five Reasons Why It Pays
to Pay Income Taxes,
and Other Special Tax Planning

Most of your clients talk to you about how to make more money and where to implement cost-reduction programs. How many clients will understand that it is important that they pay income taxes? Few! Instead, clients will ask, "Please show me how to eliminate income taxes."

This chapter shows why it is important that your service business client pay his fair share of income taxes. (I am not and never have been an Internal Revenue agent.) It contains the rationale you may present to your client to set forth the benefits to be derived by his company. Of course it will be your professional duty to help your client minimize the "income tax burden." A number of ways will also be discussed in which tax minimization can be accomplished.

It is important that the client understand why income taxes should be paid. To retain earnings in his business, your client has to pay income taxes. Business growth is sustained by earnings retained in the business. If your client operates at the zero profit level, the business cannot remain healthy. You may find that your client wants to draw out all the profit by increasing his salary. Even if you can justify to the Internal Revenue Service that such a salary is reasonable and that your client is entitled to earn that salary, you should explain to your client why earnings are important to a corporation.

1. Borrowing

First, to obtain proper credit your client needs to be able to demonstrate profitable operations. At some point in time your client will need to release his financials to a credit reporting agency such as Dun & Bradstreet, to a bank or possibly even to an important supplier. If your client wants to be able to demonstrate that the business is operating profitably, he will be forced to pay income taxes. Of course, as his tax advisor, it will be up to you to show him how to minimize income taxes. No bank will make a short-term loan nor will any insurance company make a long-term loan to your client unless he can demonstrate that he has the capability of repaying that loan. He cannot demonstrate such a capability without earning a profit and paying income taxes.

2. Renting

Second, your client will almost certainly at some point in time need to rent premises. A new landlord may insist on seeing your client's financials and/or income tax returns. Even if your client does not have to divulge his financial information, a prospective landlord may require a substantial deposit. Only if your client has generated and retained adequate earnings will such a large amount of cash be available to pay as a deposit.

3. Buying Real Estate

Third, your client may find it advantageous to acquire its own real estate. If your client seeks mortgage financing, a prospective lender will be reluctant to grant your client a proper loan to help finance the purchase if your client cannot demonstrate that its operations are profitable. Of course, the lender is primarily interested in the real estate as security for the loan. Nevertheless, a strong financial statement will make the deal much more attractive. The financial institution does not want to make a real estate loan if it believes that it may have to foreclose. Earnings and related income taxes go hand in hand.

4. Acquiring Other Companies

Fourth, your client may want to acquire another business. A profitable operation will develop the cash needed to make such an acquisition. If your client's earnings have been good, but not enough cash has been accumulated in his company, many sources of financing the acquisition from institutions will be available. Even the seller of the business may agree to take notes from your client to spread part of the purchase price over many years. All this is possible with earnings.

5. Sell Out or Go Public

Finally, your client may want to sell the business. He may want to sell all or part of it. He may want to retire or continue to work with an employment contract, full-time or part-time. He may want to "go public." He may want to merge his business. All of these goals can best be attained by having a successful business and by paying a lot of income taxes. A strong balance sheet and income statement facilitate the sale of a business. Many successful companies, because they are successful, are approached by others to make attractive deals. Capitalization of earnings is the most common arrangement in connection with the fixing of value for a business to be sold. Usually, the rule is that the stronger the financials, the greater the selling price. Many companies have difficulty selling a profitable business because profits have been deflated by the owners. Although this is usually a tax-deferred trick played by some, time catches up with this game when the owner decides to sell out.

HOW TO MINIMIZE INCOME TAXES
SUB-S

Beware of the simplistic approach that many accountants take with small businesses—Subchapter S Corporation. The Internal Revenue Code allows corporations to escape corporate income taxes by qualifying under Subchapter S. All income then flows through to the stockholder or stockholders who report the corporate profits personally. This tax minimization device is only good for the very small and not very profitable corporation. Many small businesses that employ this device should not use it for two reasons: the corporation cannot retain earnings and the client pays out too much in income tax.

HOW TO DECIDE AGAINST SUB-S

Here is a good rule-of-thumb to determine whether or not to use Sub-S: If your client's salary places him into an individual federal income tax bracket that is higher than the lowest corporate income tax bracket, then Sub-S is too costly to use. The present federal corporate income tax rate is only 17% up to $25,000 of corporate profits, and increases to 20% above that to $50,000. Above $50,000 the percentages increase. If your client's taxable income is only $7,200 after deductions and exemptions, and he is married, any additional income is taxed at the 17% rate. Therefore it does not pay to have Sub-S income above this level. Let's look at the following illustration to see how electing Subchapter S hurts your client in terms of taxes.

	A	B
Client taxable income—personal	$ 7,200	$ 7,200
Corporate taxable income (which the corporation reports as personal income of your client) Sub-S	20,000	40,000
Total	$27,200	$47,200
Federal income tax on above	$ 5,660	$14,060
Cash remaining after income tax	$21,540	$33,140

All of the corporate taxable income must be distributed to your client. None remains in the corporation. Of course your client could loan the money he receives back to the corporation, but let's see the tax effect of not using Subchapter S. The facts are the same as in the preceding example, except that the corporation pays its own federal income taxes and is an ordinary corporation —not Sub-S:

Client taxable income—personal	$ 7,200	$ 7,200
Federal income tax on above	620	620
Cash remaining after income tax	6,580	6,580
Corporate taxable income	20,000	40,000
Federal income tax on above	3,400	7,250
Cash remaining after income tax	16,600	32,750
Total cash—personal and corporate remaining after income tax	23,180	39,330
Cash savings—not using a Subchapter S	$ 1,640	$ 6,190

To recapitulate, the cash savings effected by using an ordinary corporation, not a Subchapter S corporation, in the preceding example was arrived at as follows:

	A	B
Cash remaining after your client pays his personal federal income tax using Subchapter S	$21,540	$33,140
Cash remaining after your client pays his personal federal income tax and the corporation pays its federal income tax not using Subchapter S	23,180	39,330
Cash savings	$ 1,640	$ 6,190

The cash saved will be partially in the corporation's bank account and the balance will be in your client's personal bank account, depending on the corporate earnings and the taxable income of your client. The more successful that the corporation is, the greater is the cash savings, which is really a federal income tax savings. We were recommended to a corporation that had a sole stockholder drawing a salary of $25,000 with deductions of $7,000 and his Subchapter S corporation earning $200,000. The controller of the corporation admitted that they were having difficulty in raising the cash to pay the federal income tax of the sole stockholder. The stockholder admitted that his salary of $25,000 per year was adequate for him and his family to live on. He really needed to reinvest the earnings of the corporation back into the corporation, but because of his high tax bracket he could only loan back a small percent of the corporate earnings he had to take.

CASH-BASIS TAXPAYERS: THE SECRET

The major concept that you should employ to minimize federal income taxes for your service business clients is that you should have them filing federal income tax returns on the cash basis.

The essential difference between all other types of businesses and your service business client is inventory. It is not feasible for most businesses to use the cash basis because of inventories.

By employing the cash basis, you are creating a deferral device. In other words, accrued earnings are reflected in taxable income in the next year. This has the effect of lowering earnings and related federal income taxes. Of course, the tax is ultimately paid, but there is always a lag.

For management financial reporting purposes, receivables, deferred assets and accrued liabilities should be reflected in your client's income statement, balance sheet, and statement of changes in financial position. The books of account are merely maintained on the cash basis. It should be fairly easy to accrue liabilities as well as set up deferrals on the balance sheet dates. Income should similarly be accrued. After a cash-basis general ledger trial balance is taken off, a worksheet should be prepared on which all accruals and deferrals should be recorded. Usually at the end of each month, the journal entries for accruals and deferrals can be standardized into a recurring entry system so that only the amounts need be inserted on the worksheet each month. If your client has a full-time bookkeeper, you should train that person to prepare the worksheet and recurring journal entries each month. You may go one step further and train the bookkeeper to prepare monthly financials, if you believe that the bookkeeper is capable. Then all you need to do each month is to review the adjustments and check to assure yourself that the financials have been prepared correctly for management.

FIVE RULES-OF-THUMB FOR DETERMINING HOW MUCH SALARY YOUR CLIENT SHOULD PAY HIMSELF

You should be able to tell your client how much to pay himself. Even if your client does not ask you that question, you should ask it. Why? There are two reasons. First, you will be called upon to justify the salary of your client when his corporation is audited by the Internal Revenue Service (IRS)—and if you want to retain your client you had better be prepared to explain your client's position to satisfy the agent. Second, as the accountant and financial advisor, you should be able to determine the ability of the business to pay your client a reasonable salary.

There are several rules-of-thumb to apply in determining what to tell your client when you discuss his salary with him. Let's assume that your client is both the president of his corporation and its controlling stockholder.

Rule One

Find out how much your client needs simply to live as he would like or has been accustomed to earning. This amount, for all practical purposes, he will need to draw as a minimum.

Rule Two

Find out what others are earning in similar circumstances. Many published studies of executive compensation are available such as trade association or industry groups. The Robert Morris Associates annually publish statement studies which list officers' salaries as a percentage of net sales. The size and complexity of your client's business, as well as the responsibilities assumed by your client, are the guidelines for his salary. During the 1950's and 1960's, the IRS generally used a rule-of-thumb of five percent (5%) of net sales. If your client's corporation is grossing $1,000,000 in sales volume, using this rule, a salary of $50,000 per year would probably be reasonable.

Rule Three

Find how much the client's corporation can afford to pay. Here you have to be very careful. Remember that if you fail to determine the ability of the company to pay a reasonable salary at the beginning of the fiscal year, you may face a "dividend" problem at the end of the fiscal year. This problem arises when your client tells you at the end of the fiscal year that business was good and he wants a bonus. If you accede to this request, the IRS may contend that the so-called bonus was a "dividend." The Internal Revenue agent could disallow the deduction, maintaining that the bonus was in fact an additional distribution of corporate earnings, not a bonus as intended. One solution is to try to avoid year-end bonuses. If your client is not a controlling stockholder, you can overcome this situation by having the directors set up a bonus plan at the beginning of the fiscal year related to salaries and profits. If your client is a controlling stockholder and you have determined that there is not enough cash available during the fiscal year to pay him his full salary, you should accrue the full salary throughout the fiscal year. Seventy-five days after the year is over, the Internal Revenue Code requires that the undrawn salary be paid or your client may not deduct it on the corporate tax return. In certain cases, your client might pay himself and loan part of that accrual back to the company if it needs the cash. Of course interest should be accrued and paid on this loan.

Rule Four

Be sure that your client, even if he is the sole stockholder of the corporation, has an employment contract with the corporation. Usually the corporate minutes recite the officers' salaries early in the fiscal year. This tactic helps substantiate the deduction.

Rule Five

Have a rational basis for increasing your client's salary from one year to the next. For example, if the corporation has a union and has agreed to pay a 10% cost-of-living increase to union employees, certainly your client should be able to get a 10% increase. Even if your client has no union or if he increases his unionized employees at only 5% or 6%, you can get a higher raise for him. Analyze the salary increases he gives to his key employees. Many times these valuable people are promoted with substantial annual increases. For example, if your client has a $30,000-a-year sales manager who is raised to $35,000, your client could raise his salary commensurately from $75,000 per annum to $87,500. Of course, if the sales manager happens to be your client's son, then the rationale is tainted because it is no longer arm's-length. You have to prove "reasonable" compensation. If the sales manager is the minority stockholder, be careful that the two stockholders do not raise their salaries in proportion to their stockholdings, which could appear to be a dividend distribution.

HOW TO DEAL WITH THE UNREASONABLE ACCUMULATION OF EARNINGS PITFALL

Section 531 of the present Internal Revenue Code imposes a tax on unreasonable accumulation of earnings when retained earnings exceed $150,000. The tax is not imposed on the retained earnings but on the net income or "taxable income" of the corporation for the year or years being audited by the IRS.

All of your successful corporate clients are vulnerable under Section 531 when their retained earnings exceed $150,000, unless they can demonstrate that earnings are reinvested in the corporation or are distributed to the stockholders in the form of dividends.

The regulations and cases relating to Section 531 are complex and changing. Nevertheless, you should be aware that the IRS has a problem applying Section 531 to service businesses. Briefly, the problem lies in the IRS's use of the "Bardahl Formula." You will find in many IRS audits that the Internal Revenue agent will take out his formula and try to calculate whether or not your service business client is accumulating earnings or putting the earnings into working capital.

We know that there is no working capital in a service business, but the IRS does not recognize this fact. The courts have been wrestling with this problem since July 1965, when the U.S. Tax Court handed down its landmark decision in *Bardahl Manufacturing Corp.* (24 Tax Court Memo 1030, 1965). Bardahl was not a service business, but in 1975 the Tax Court applied its formula in *W. L. Mead, Inc.* Although the Court modified the original formula, it nevertheless assumed that *Bardahl* was applicable. Therefore, you will have to live with this decision unless you want to challenge it in the Courts. It is recommended that you go through the *Bardahl* calculation to determine the vulnerability of your client. Be sure that you can prove that your client is reinvesting his earnings in the business. Reinvestment usually takes the form of plant, property and equipment in a service business. Some service corporations also solve this problem by acquiring related businesses. It is important that your client document his corporate reinvestment activities by recording such efforts in the corporate minutes. Even if his corporation does not reinvest in a given year, its search and attempt to acquire will be recognized by the IRS, but be careful. Of course, ultimately your client will have to acquire, reinvest or declare dividends.

THE "SILENT PARTNER"

One approach that you may express to your client is that he has a "silent partner"—the Government. At all times he must operate his business in recognition of that fact. Always assume he will be audited by the IRS and tell that to him.

HOW TO SELECT THE BEST TAX VEHICLE

Certain service businesses lend themselves to the partnership rather than corporate form including personal services and real estate investment. Tax and economic considerations are paramount. For example, investors form partnerships in anticipation of appreciation of their real estate or because their operations will result in a tax loss in early years. If the investment is sound, mortgage debt is increased in later years giving rise to "tax-free income." Of course there is no real "income," but there is a real cash flow into your client's personal pocket without a dividend problem.

Partnerships avoid other corporate tax traps such as Section 531 as well as provide flexibility of capital flow into or out of the partnership. Additional partners may enter or leave without adverse income tax consequences.

You should decide and recommend the most favorable tax entity to your service business client/company. Be sure your client/company obtains proper legal advice before selecting the entity. There may be more significant reasons such as limitation of liabilities which may control the decision to incorporate.

TO SUM UP

1. It will pay off over the years if your client is able to pay income taxes to be able to:

    a) borrow
    b) rent
    c) buy real estate
    d) acquire other companies
    e) sell out
    f) merge
    g) go "public"

2. Be careful to minimize the tax your client will pay. The major concept to employ in tax deferral is "cash basis" filing.

3. You should determine the "best" salary for your client and tell him why.

4. Beware that your client is not trapped by Section 531 of the Internal Revenue Code (unreasonable accumulation of earnings.) Be sure that your client reinvests earnings and acquires or declares dividends.

5. Select the best tax vehicle to operate the business.

9

How to Prepare and Set Up Effective Service Business Budgets

Most service businessmen overlook one of the best tools available to develop and control their operations—a budget. A budget is a two-sided coin, one aspect concerns itself with a profit plan, and the other concerns itself with a cash plan. In other words, a budget should have two goals—income statement goals and balance sheet goals. To do this, your client needs to create two budgets. A cash budget is needed for planning and controlling those activities relating to acquisition and disposal of fixed assets, acquisition and amortization of debt, investment activity, and dividend policy. An operations budget is needed to plan and control the day-to-day management of the service business to create and maintain profitable operations. The two budgets are tied together by the net income from the operations budget. This chapter explains how to prepare and set up budgets as well as to set forth how budgets can best be used. The reason why cash budgets and operational budgets must both be prepared is simple. Your client could prepare a very profitable operational budget and still go bankrupt or struggle with a severe shortage of cash. By setting up balance sheet goals, your client will plan to live within the restrictions placed on his business on the cash available from operations. If the cash budget demonstrates that more cash will be used than is generated from operations, your client will know that additional cash must be provided to fund his business from outside sources. If for some reason he is unable to obtain this cash from outside the business, he will have to adjust both his cash budget and operational budget so that total cash available, as forecast, will be adequate to keep the operations running. The business may also have a seasonality when cash receipts fall. A proper cash budget should provide for this seasonality so that adequate cash reserves are accumulated prior to the period when cash receipts fall or lines of credit are arranged in advance of cash needs unless it is feasible to defer certain types of unusual cash disbursements when cash receipts fall.

THREE-PHASE IMPLEMENTATION OF THE BUDGETARY PROCESS

The first and most important step in implementing the budgetary process is to involve management. Beware of the client who tells you to go back to your office, prepare a budget, and come back to him. If you follow those instructions, the budgetary process will fail, because it is essential that management be involved step-by-step from the inception. It is important that you explain to your client that it is his budget which he must create (you can help in the creation) and which he must use to control his business. The danger is that if you do all the work, it will be your budget, not your client's. You may have to sell him the idea that budgeting is useful and profitable.

PHASE ONE

Let's get to the heart of budgeting. The best way to start is by projecting gross income or sales. Only your client should do this. When you ask the first question in the budgetary process—"What will be your sales?"—you are forcing him to think about his future operations (i.e., "What will sales be next month, next quarter, or next year?")

In some service businesses, especially in personal services, the first question may be, "What do the partners want to earn next year?" Then, "How do they go about earning what they want?"

You may help your client answer the first question. If your client says, "How should I know how much my sales will be next month or next year?" you should use a common-sense approach. Use the historical past as a guide: What happened last year (by month and by quarter)? What has happened during the current year to change the anticipated sales this coming year? What has your client done internally which will have an effect on this coming year's sales? How much will external factors, direct and indirect, have an effect on this coming year's sales? For example, if your client is in a personal service business, he may project only an increase slightly better than the factor of inflation. All you need do for him is to suggest that he multiply last year's fees by an anticipated rate of inflation, say, seven or eight percent. If your client is an attorney and he grossed $100,000 last year, he could forecast fees of $108,000 next year. This "guesstimating" or forecasting of sales is the real beginning of the budgetary process. If your client is a law firm with three partners, all three should meet. Each should prepare his own forecast of anticipated fees, those he expects to bill clients as well as those he expects to collect from clients. At a meeting of the partners, a forecast should be made by the firm of collections and anticipated services or billings. If your client owns a radio station, the sales manager, assisted by the salesmen, should forecast sales. Each salesman should analyze each customer to forecast how much advertising service he expects to produce during the next fiscal year. The sales manager should review and revise these budgets to prepare a station sales budget for submission and final review to the general manager or owner. Of course, no one really knows what the sales will be, but that is no justification for failure to forecast.

PRICING

Whether your client is a law firm, a radio station owner or in some other service business, a decision must be made as to pricing. The lawyers must decide what they want to charge for their time, just as the radio station operator or owner must decide on rate changes. Three factors play a role in the decision—what has been charged in the past, what the competition is charging and what your client believes he can charge in the future. At the least, a review of pricing should be done annually. In some businesses, prices are adjusted quarterly. The frequency depends on the nature of the business as well as the rate of inflation that your client expects. Be sure to remind your client that he will have to pay higher wages and nearly all of his other costs and expenses will increase during the next year before he makes the pricing decisions. Most personal service businesses charge fees based on the annual salary of the staff man or partner providing the service. To illustrate, a staff attorney or accountant earning an $18,000-a-year salary may be billed out by the law firm or accounting firm at a multiple of salary. Assuming 1,800 hours per year, the hourly rate charged could vary from 2.5 to 3 times hourly salary. In this illustration, the rate would be $10.00 per hour times 2.5 or $25.00 per hour. Some firms may charge $30.00 per hour or more for the same staff man. The salary multiple depends on the overhead and profit to be allocated to the hourly staff rate. Many professionals also charge clerical time to their clients in a manner similar to staff and partner charges. No matter what charges are determined, your client must be competitive in his pricing. He must recover his cost and still make a profit or he will be out of business. Too many professionals such as doctors, dentists, attorneys, and yes, even CPAs, are not good businessmen. They may set fair fees and neglect to review them. Here is where the budgetary process helps. It is a constant reminder.

PHASE TWO

Once income forecasts have been made, the next step in the budgetary process is to forecast expenses. There are two approaches to expense forecasting. The best approach is to forecast the operational needs of the company and to quantify each need as to its expense. An easier approach is to review past expenses and determine what will be required to run the company during the next year, assuming that the budget period is the year.

Forecasting business needs should be done by bottom-level supervisors and reviewed by the owners or the general manager. Again, you could be present at any point in this process. For example, in a radio station, the sales manager should project next year's expenses, explaining in detail how much it will cost him to run his department. He may need you to either help him prepare or review his estimates.

Reviewing past expenses and determining what will be required to operate the company is the easier approach, and it should also be done by bottom-level supervisors. To perform this function, each supervisor should have a copy of his department's portion of the income statement for the prior period. The owners or general manager should evaluate the supervisor's budget with his financial advisors as well as his outside accountants. Each supervisor's budget becomes part of the total company budget.

It is also important that each function be quantified; for instance, how many people will be needed and what each person will do as well as the cost of that person directly and indirectly. Since payroll and related costs are the major elements in nearly all service businesses, control over these items will provide the most significant pay-back to improve efficiency and profitability.

When the operational budget is complete, it should look like an income statement except that it is for the year ahead, not for the year just ended. Most operational budgets are further broken down into monthly and quarterly columns. Usually it is significant to have monthly budgets for two reasons—change and control. Expenses will vary from month to month, and therefore the budget will be changing. Even expenses which seem to be relatively fixed will vary from time to time. Also, monthly budgeting affords a time frame for reasonable control. At the end of each month, budgeted expenses can be compared with the actual expenses incurred. Expense overruns can be spotted and analyzed before it is too late for action. Furthermore, if a supervisor plans to exceed his budget in any given month, he can discuss his problems with top-level management before the decision is made to incur expenses which will exceed planned amounts.

Let's be specific. Assume payroll overtime is budgeted at $10,000 in the program department of a radio station in January. However, the department manager has a problem and wants to spend $19,000, which he believes will be needed to do the work and solve the problem. If he had previously been given authority to exceed his budget by twelve percent (12%), then he knows that if he authorizes spending of $19,000 in January, he will exceed his budget by $9,000. He only has authority to spend $10,000 plus 12%, or $11,200 in January. Therefore, he must get advance permission to exceed his monthly budget by $7,800 ($19,000 — $11,200).

When the completed budget is evaluated by top management,

the total corporate plan becomes visible and each department must be judged as part of the whole business.

PHASE THREE

Activity budgets are prepared by many businesses for certain phases of operations. These are special budgets which may be recurring or non-recurring. For instance, the sales department of a radio station may prepare an advertising budget or a promotion budget. The promotion budget may cover a specific one-shot promotion or a promotional campaign. Some promotional budgets can be set up yearly and broken down by month with specific items forecast to occur in certain months during the year. Again, the activity budget will be detailed to include all possible costs and expenses. Some activities may be permanent such as research and development. What we are really saying is that a budget may be prepared for certain categories of expense. Another example is a training budget. Your client may project a training expense for the year of $50,000. Then he may have prepared a detailed schedule of what comprises the $50,000. It should look like the following:

ILLUSTRATION #1

TRAINING BUDGET

	Oct.	Nov.	Dec.	Total
Books, periodicals and other materials	6,400	3,000	4,200	$13,600
Reproducing costs	400	300	300	1,000
Payroll and fringe costs	4,900	4,900	4,900	14,700
Seminars—Outside, all costs	7,100	5,500	2,200	14,800
Seminars—Inside, fees	1,000	500	4,400	5,900
Total Training Budget	$19,800	$14,200	$16,000	$50,000

In Illustration #1, all of the training costs and expenses were budgeted for the three months ended December 31. In the income statement in October, on the line for Training Expense, was the budgeted amount of only $19,800. The details did not appear in the income statement. When the actual expenses were incurred during the three months ended December 31, they were recorded in the income statement as follows in Illustration #2.

ILLUSTRATION #2

TRAINING EXPENSE

	October Actual	October Budget	November Actual	November Budget	December Actual	December Budget
Books, Periodicals and Other Materials ..	$ 5,700	$ 6,400	$ 3,100	$ 3,000	$ 4,500	$ 4,200
Reproducing Costs	600	400	300	300	400	300
Payroll and fringe costs	4,800	4,900	4,800	4,900	4,800	4,900
Seminars— Outside, all costs	6,500	7,100	5,500	5,500	2,400	2,200
Seminars— Inside, fees	1,000	1,000	500	500	4,400	4,400
Totals	$18,600	$19,800	$14,200	$14,200	$16,500	$16,000

Many businesses would have one additional column each month to indicate the variance from actual to budgeted amount. When the months are spread across as in Illustration #2, there is a tendency to omit the variance column in order that the trend may be more easily observed as expenses are reported from month to month. Let's look at the month of October, using the variance concept as set forth in Illustration #3:

ILLUSTRATION #3

TRAINING EXPENSE

	October Actual	October Budget	October Variance Under (Over)
Books, Periodicals and Other Materials	$ 5,700	$ 6,400	$ 700
Reproducing Costs	600	400	(200)
Payroll and Fringe Costs	4,800	4,900	100
Seminars—Outside, all costs	6,500	7,100	600
Seminars—Inside, fees	1,000	1,000	—
Totals	$18,600	$19,800	$1,200

BALANCE SHEET GOALS OR CASH BUDGETS

While the operational budget is being prepared throughout the company, the financial people (and this could involve the outside accountants) should be preparing a cash budget. This procedure is much simpler than the procedure required to prepare the operational budget because the cash estimated to be received and to be expended is based on the forecast of revenues as well as expenses to be incurred. Revenues are translated into cash collections based on anticipated average collection days. Payments for payroll and all other expense categories can be projected based on the operational budget. Then debt service requirements and all liability payments such as withholding taxes are entered into the forecast of cash to be disbursed. This is done month by month. Where cash receipts are exceeded by cash disbursements, it becomes apparent that your client will have to borrow or reduce cash disbursements. The safest way to do cash budgeting is to do it weekly until an adequate cash balance is set aside as a reserve. Some companies like to have at least one month's normal cash disbursments set aside as a reserve. Then cash budgeting could be done monthly because weekly imbalances could be handled from the cash reserve.

The only major information that the cash budget does not obtain from the operational budget relates to acquisition of fixed assets; investments in and advances to affiliates or subsidiaries; debt amortization; dividend policy; and payments of non-expenses or non-cost type liabilities such as taxes withheld, including payroll taxes withheld, sales taxes and so on. All of these transactions must be projected in the cash budget. Total cost of fixed assets to be acquired in the next year must be forecast by top management. Future loans, investments and dividends fall within the discretion and authority of top management. Before preparing a cash budget, you must be sure that top management (with your guidance, if necessary) reviews and forecasts what may be classified as balance sheet goals relating to the items just enumerated.

Cash budgets take the form of receipts and disbursements schedules. Receipts arise in the normal course of business as collections of receivables. Unusual receipts include borrowing and proceeds of sales of assets not in the normal course of business. All of these transactions must be forecast and placed into the cash budget. Disbursements include payments for all expenses and taxes as well as payments of all liabilities, purchases of fixed assets, investments in and advances to others, and payments of dividends.

Proper forecasting of cash flows will affect many top-level decisions. For example, adequate cash flow will be a factor determining whether to buy or lease fixed assets. In personal service businesses, cash flow will be a factor in determining profit distributions to partners and staff.

See Chapter 3, Illustration #7 for details of a cash budget for a semi-annual period, an explanation of cash flow, how to analyze it and how to control it. Comparing actual cash flow with the budget is the ultimate tool in tracking the business from period to period.

FORECASTING FOR THE NEW BUSINESS

It is much more difficult to prepare operational budgets and cash budgets for the new business. There are no historical guidelines and no prior period experiences.

The first step is to estimate capital requirements and identify the source or sources of the capital needed. Then future income must be estimated at least one year in advance. Next, all expenses must be anticipated for the budget year. At this point, an operational budget takes shape.

The second step is to prepare a cash budget by week, month, quarters and for the year. Collections and disbursements must be forecast.

At the end of the first month of operation of the business, both the operational budget and cash budget should be reviewed and revised if necessary. Each month this procedure should be repeated until adequate cash reserves are set aside for unexpected disbursements or unanticipated collection problems. The first year is usually the most difficult. In the second year of a new business, at least there is the original budget to use as a guide.

ZERO-BASED BUDGETING IN A NUTSHELL

A common-sense approach to the budgeting process is simply to take a hard look at last year's expenses and ask, "Can this expense be eliminated or replaced?" or "Can this function be adjusted to reduce the expense in next year's budget?" There is a great tendency to keep doing the same thing, especially if the business is operating successfully. Because many service businesses are not subject to the swift changes of obsolescence, they fail to see the gradual changes occurring in their fields. Zero-based budgeting, with its questioning demands, forces reassessment of each line in the operational budget or each line in last year's income statement. An appraisal must be made at least annually of each cost of doing business when your client uses the concept of zero-based budgeting to arrive at his income statement goals.

Balance sheet goals should also be reviewed annually, but the questions are slightly different: "Is there a better way, cheaper or more efficient, to finance the business?" "Is it time to replace or sell off assets?" "Can amortization charges be reduced?" "Should the present balance sheet structure be altered or can it be altered?"

One of the interesting facets of zero-based budgeting is the requirement that all questions be answered in writing. There must be written justification of each decision to keep or get rid of a particular expense or cost.

TO SUM UP

1. Budgets are control tools for your client. He should prepare and set up two kinds—the operational budget and the cash budget.

2. Budgets are implemented by involving management. The first step is to estimate sales or revenues at future prices or rates. The second step is to forecast expenses. All levels of management should participate in the forecasting process.

3. Some activities should be budgeted separately such as advertising or training. Actual expenses and income should be compared monthly with budgeted amounts.

4. Another task is to employ zero-based budgeting. This approach requires questioning the rationale behind each item of expense and justifying every cost which will go into next year's budget.

5. A balance sheet budget should be forecast to anticipate all assets and liabilities.

6. Finally, cash budgets involving receipts and disbursements should be prepared by forecasting collections and payments.

10

Financial Tools Usually Overlooked but Needed to Build a Profitable Service Organization

A business is only as good as its people. This is especially true of service businesses, where inventory is not a factor in producing revenues. Personal service businesses comprise the largest single category of service businesses. In fact, there are more varieties of personal service businesses than all other kinds of service businesses combined.

Financial tools are needed to build a proper organization. To motivate employees and develop a successful service business, your client should be prepared to offer a financial package as well as an environment that is conducive to efficiency and productivity. Too often your client will believe that salary is the sole factor in the financial package. Actually, there are two additional factors to be added to the salary factor. These are the incentive factor and the non-salary payment or fringe benefits.

INCENTIVE PLANS

In addition to salary, employees are motivated by incentive plans of which there are two basic types: plans which reward performances that exceed standards or goals and plans which reward discoveries or unusual specific accomplishments. Bonus plans are common incentive plans to reward performance by employees who are paid specific amounts when goals are exceeded. This is a good financial tool, but be careful. If your client's bonus plan rewards stockholder-employees in control of the business, the IRS may claim that the bonus is really a dividend. If the employee recipient is not a controlling stockholder, there is no taint or suggestion of dividends. Here the bonus is a wage supplement. The plan should be in writing. If your client is a sole stockholder and pays himself an incentive bonus, then he places himself into a difficult posture in relation to taxes. The bonus looks like a dividend. Why would a sole stockholder need an incentive bonus at all? If his salary is fair and reasonable, it is quite simple to cause the directors to declare a dividend (assuming the client controls his board of directors). If your client is a corporation with a group of stockholders where a bonus has been set up for the president who is only a minority stockholder, the plan is obviously an incentive supplement to his salary. Some plans even give the president additional compensation in the form of a percentage of pre-tax earnings or some other arm's-length formula for incentive.

Beneficial suggestions or recommendations are rewarded by bonuses or other incentive payments. Unusual specific accomplishments such as discoveries or major task accomplishments should be rewarded by incentive plans. Usually a dollar value is set on the specific achievement. For example, if employees suggest changes or tactics that result in cost savings to the company, the employee should be given a cash bonus. The fact that such a plan is in existence should be communicated to all employees. When bonuses are paid to deserving individuals, the company should exploit that fact by communicating it to all other employees.

FRINGE BENEFITS

The financial package would not be complete without fringe benefits or non-cash payments made by the corporation to provide incentives to employees. Each situation has to be tailored to fit the company and its people. Rewards, or, as the British call them, "perks," depend upon the goals of the company, its size, and the level of the employee. Some fringes have become so customary and routine that almost all employees expect them. These include medical and health insurance plans. Group life insurance is becoming more commonplace. Some companies even set up medical expense reimbursement plans. If the employee is expected to travel, the corporation may purchase or lease an automobile, which may be considered a fringe benefit. Many companies conduct employee training programs and seminars at resorts, with all expenses paid by the corporation. The list could go on and on. Be careful that your client complies, however, with all of the regulations and provisions of the Internal Revenue Code. Do not allow your client to reward himself to the exclusion of other employees. You will have to defend the deduction in an examination by the Internal Revenue Service. Laws, regulations, rulings and cases keep changing in this area. Stay current. Do not let your client overreach himself to provide fringe benefits. Always assume that he will be audited by the IRS. Be sure that he operates his business under that assumption. Remember that your small service business client considers you, his outside accountant, as his "tax expert."

PENSION PLANS

Another financial tool your service business client can utilize is a pension plan. These plans fall into two categories—IRS approved and qualified under the Internal Revenue Code and non-IRS approved. Both types of plans are deductible. The difference arises in the funding. Qualified plans are those wherein the corporation makes a payment into a fund. The amount of the payment is determined actuarially. The payment is immediately deductible by the corporation. When employees retire, at some later date, the fund pays out in the form of a pension or lump sum to the employee. Many pension plans include life insurance coverage for the employees. When the plan is not qualified, only direct pension payments are deductible by the corporation. Your client will probably prefer a qualified plan which has the advantage of accumulating funds in a tax-exempt vehicle until the monies are needed to pay employees at retirement. The pension plan is another area of the Internal Revenue Code that is continually changing. As long as your client does not discriminate in favor of stockholder-employees, there may be a significant tax benefit for him in a pension plan. Care must be taken in setting up such a plan. In the final analysis, the company must be able to afford the cost of a pension plan.

PROFIT-SHARING PLANS

The financial package would not be complete without a presentation of the profit-sharing plan concept. Before we begin, it should be pointed out that such a plan does not require divulging of financial information to employees who participate in a profit-sharing plan. No employee need be told how much the corporation earned when a profit-sharing plan is in existence. All that the employee need know is how much is being put into the plan's fund for him and how much was earned for his account in the fund as well as the details of his account.

There are also two categories of profit-sharing plans—IRS-approved or qualified and non-IRS-approved. Most plans are qualified. The principal difference between qualified profit-sharing plans and qualified pension plans is that the pension plan has an actuarially computed goal for each employee whereas there is no such fixed goal required for the profit-sharing plan.

The qualified profit-sharing plan allows the corporation to set aside part of its profit into a tax-exempt fund for future payment to employees. Each employee who participates in the plan shares usually based on formula tied to salary. Plans may not discriminate in favor of stockholder-employees.

The non-IRS-qualified profit-sharing plans do not permit payments into a tax-exempt fund. They usually require direct payments to employees in order to be deductible.

PHANTOM STOCK PLAN

Another type of profit-sharing plan is the "phantom stock plan," which is non-qualified. This type of plan is suitable for clients who want key employees to share earnings but do not want to give up ownership in the corporation or declare dividends. As long as your client is willing to divulge earnings, he can give away phantom stock. Actually, the corporation enters into a contract whereby the named employee is granted additional compensation, which gives rise to a theoretical share of stock ownership. The contract varies from company to company, and the recipients may consider themselves stockholders. No cash is paid out at the time of the grant and no tax deduction arises until the corporation actually makes cash payment. Usually payments are not made for many years or are made at retirement. Let's illustrate the phantom stock plan. Your client has a key employee to whom he is willing to divulge earnings and net worth. Assume a corporate net worth of $1,000,000, as shown in Illustration #1.

ILLUSTRATION #1

X CORPORATION

PHANTOM STOCK PLAN

Net Worth	$1,000,000.00
Phantom shares or units	1,000,000
Value per unit	$1.00
Units granted (by contract)	25,000
Value of units granted	$ 25,000.00

Date of grant—January 1, 19XX
  (usually first day of fiscal year)
Employee-participant—John P. Jones
            Executive Vice President

In Illustration #1, your client has caused his corporation, X Corporation, to enter into a contract with John P. Jones, executive vice-president, to grant him 25,000 units on January 1, 19XX. Jones will share in the growth of the corporation from that date forward. For example, if the net worth has increased from $1,000,000 to $1,100,000 on January 1, 19XX one year later, due to an increase in retained earnings, Jones' 25,000 units will have grown in value from $1.00 to approximately $1.07. The value has been arived at by dividing the new net worth of $1,100,000 by 1,025,000 units at fiscal year-end. The value of Jones' share in the corporation will increase with earnings. When Jones retires, or at some stipulated date, the corporation must pay Jones the computed value. This payment will be compensation to Jones and will then be tax deducted by the corporation. The accrued value of $25,000 must be deductible for accounting purposes and set up on the balance sheet as a deferred liability. The principal disadvantage to phantom stock plans is the fact that earnings are charged and there is no related income tax deduction at the time of the charge.

TO SUM UP

To conclude, there is a group of financial tools usually overlooked but needed to build an organization. These include incentive plans to reward performance or achievement, fringe benefits or non-cash income supplements such as health insurance or a corporate automobile, plans to share profits or create future rights to pensions and plans to give the appearance of stock ownership such as phantom stock plans.

Index